Master, from........................of........................

Arrived..

Packages and Goods	Consignee	Delivered
to London	light	12 : 1 : 51.
to Colchester		
Wheat .	arrived	16 : 1 : 51.
to London .	light	31 : 1 : 51.
to Colchester		
Wheat	arrived	7 : 2 : 51.
to Felixstowe		
Wheat	arrived	1 : 3 : 51.
to London	Light	4 : 3 : 51.
to Ipswich		
potash	arrived	13 : 3 : 51.
London	light	20 : 3 : 51.
to Ipswich		
Maize	arrived	27 : 3 : 51.
London	Light	3 : 4 : 51.
Rochford .		
Wheat	arrived .	17 . 4 . 51.

LONDON LIGHT
A Sailorman's Story

An Autobiography by
Jim Lawrence

CHAFFCUTTER

Cover picture: At the wheel of **Memory**, when bound Felixstowe for London, 1956.

Endpapers: Sailing barge Log Book recording passages, including those to 'London Light'.

Chaffcutter Books, 39 Friars Road, Braughing, Ware, Hertfordshire, SG11 2NN, U.K.

Printed and bound by Gomer Press Limited, Llandysul Enterprise Park, Llandysul, Ceredigion, SA44 4JL, U.K.

CONTENTS

To Pauline, who has shared my love of the the water.

Picture Sources

Some of the images included are from the author's personal collection gathered over 60+ years. Unsurprisingly, the origins of some have been lost with the passage of time and those falling into this category are listed as from the Author's Coll. (Collection). Duplicates of certain photos have been provided by different people. The best of these have been used, credited to that provider.

Where known, the name of the photographer appears first, followed by source details, latest information last. Positions within the book are indicated by page number, and image position where more than one photograph appears on a single page.

Front cover: Photo, Barry Pearce; 9: Author's Coll.; 10: Barry Pearce; 13: Photo, Richard Walsh.; 14: Ray Rush Coll.; 17: Author's Coll.; 21: Ray Rush Coll.; 23 top: Photo, Alan Cordell; 23 bottom: Photo, Ralph Merry, Authors Coll.; 24, 25: Barry Pearce Coll.; 26: Alf Pyner Coll., S.S.B.R.; 27: Frank Thompson Coll., S.S.B.R.; 28: Alan Cameron Coll., S.S.B.R.; 29: Mersea Museum; 31: Hervey Benham Coll., Mersea Museum; 32: Ron Green Coll., Mersea Museum; 33: John White Coll.; 34: Ron Green Coll., Mersea Museum; 36: Rick Hogben Coll., S.S.B.R.; 37: Hervey Benham Coll., Mersea Museum; 38 top: Photo, Douglas Went, Barry Pearce Coll.; 38 bottom, 39 left: Author's Coll.; 39 right: Arthur Bennett Coll., S.S.B.R.; 40: Author's Coll.; 41: Richard Walsh Coll.; 42: Photo, Aubrey Frost, Ken & Carol Greenhalgh Coll.; 44: Ray Rush Coll.; 46 top: Photo, Arthur Bennett, S.S.B.R.; 46 bottom: Photo, Lucy Harris; 47: Author's Coll.; 49: Arthur Bennett Coll., S.S.B.R.; 50: Photo, Ted Kemp, Robert Kemp Coll.; 51: Photoship.com; 52: Barry Pearce Coll.; 53: Peter Dodds Coll.; 54: John Horner Coll.; 55 top & bottom: Barry Pearce Coll.; 57: Barry Pearce Coll.; 58: Author's Coll.; 59: National Maritime Museum; 61: Maritime Photo Agency; 62: Author's Coll.; 64: Barry Pearce Coll.; 66: S.S.B.R.; 68: Richard Walsh Coll.; 70: Barry Pearce Coll.; 71: Author's Coll.; 72: Peter Dodds Coll.; 74: Hervey Benham Coll., S.S.B.R.; 75: Author's Coll.; 76: Photo, John Leggatt, Author's Coll.; 77: Photo, John Hargreaves, Peter Dodds Coll.; 78: Author's Coll.; 79, 80, 81 & 82: Graham Hussey Coll., Ipswich Maritime Trust; 83 top & bottom: Photos, Lucy Harris; 84: Photo, Roger Finch, Barry Pearce Coll.; 85: Photo, Bill Dean, Author's Coll.; 86: Photo, Les Arnold, Alan Cordell Coll.; 87: Author's Coll.; 88: Photo, S.J. Shipman, S.S.B.R.; 89 & 90 top: S.S.B.R.; 90 bottom: Jack Jeffs Coll., S.S.B.R.; 91: Author's Coll.; 92: Photo, Will Middleton Coll., S.S.B.R.; 93: Photo, Ralph Merry; 95 top: Photo, Mick Lungley; 95 bottom: Photo, Les Sadler; 97: National Historic Ships, U.K.; 98: Photo, Paul Plumridge; 99: Photo, John Fairbrother; 100: Photo, John Hargreaves; 103: S.S.B.R.; 104: Author's Coll.; 106 top: Photo, Barry Pearce; 106 bottom: Author's Coll.; 107: Author's Coll.; 108: Ray Rush Coll.; 111: Graham Dent Coll.; 114: Graham Hussey Coll., Ipswich Maritime Trust; 116: Topsail Charters Coll.; 118: Graham Hussey Coll., Ipswich Maritime Trust; 121: Jack Jeffs Coll., S.S.B.R.; 123: Author's Coll.; 125 top: Ray Rush Coll.; 125 bottom: Author's Coll.; 128 top: Hervey Benham Coll., Mersea Museum; 128 bottom: Photo, Michael Lobb; 130: Jack Jeffs Coll., S.S.B.R.; 132: John Fairbrother Coll.; 133: Author's Coll.; 135: Richard Walsh Coll.; 136 top: Author's Coll.; 136 bottom: Photo, Arthur Bennett, S.S.B.R.; 137: Author's Coll.; 138: Museum of London P.L.A. Coll.; 139: Photo, Arthur Bennett, S.S.B.R.; 141: Photo, John Fairbrother; 143: Drawing, Lucy Harris; 144: Charles Traill Coll.; 145: Jack Jeffs Coll., S.S.B.R.; 146: John Clarkson Coll., Ships in Focus; 147: Neil Cox Coll., www.ourgreatyarmouth.org.uk; 148 top: Photo, David Miller, Richard Smith Coll., S.S.B.R.; 148 bottom & 149 top: Author's Coll.; 149 bottom: David Hocquard Coll.; 150: Barry Pearce Coll.; 151: Author's Coll.; 152: Museum of London P.L.A. Coll.; 154: Author's Coll.; 155: Photo, Austin Farrar, Author's Coll.; 157: Robert Simper Coll.; 158: Photo, Ken Chamberlain; 160: Photo, Steve Worrell; 161, 162, 165 top & bottom: Author's Coll.; 167 top: Photo, Author; 167 bottom: Author's Coll.; 168 top: Colin Swindale Coll.; 168 bottom: Photo, John Parrish; 169, 171: Author's Coll.; 173 top: J.E. Kemp archive; 173 bottom: Author's Coll.; 174: Photo, Basil Emmerson; 175, 176, 177, 178 & 179: Author's Coll.; 180: Sea Cloud Cruises, Hamburg; 181 top & bottom: Author's Coll.; 183: Photo, Robert Simper; 185 top: Author's Coll.; 185 bottom: Lucy Harris Coll.; 186: Photo, Brian Webb; 187: Author's Coll.; 188: Photo, Peter Scott.

ACKNOWLEDGEMENTS

My sincere thanks to Margo and Keith Starkey, for making me write down my memories and for the many hours they spent, albeit with much fun and laughter, in typing and correcting and making it into readable matter – a huge task. To Richard Walsh, for his input and extreme care over the design and production of this book, and seeing that the whole thing made perfect sense; and to Lucy Harris for correlating and editing the typescript, plus other help.

My grateful thanks go to many of the ex-professionals who have lent a hand: Ray Rush, for making his entire picture collection available to me; bargeman and artist Barry Pearce and John Fairbrother, who took more trouble than me to take photographs at the time. Thanks also to 'Paddy' O'Driscoll, a great contributor to the history of the working barges; Mick Lungley, who was always willing to share his knowledge with new barge crew and, of course, Rick Cardy, a very special friend, and barge mate during the early chartering days.

I would also like to thank David Patient, shipwright, historian and member of the 'permanent staff'; also Colin Swindale, a storehouse of knowledge. Don Wright was very helpful with digging out pictures preserved in the S.S.B.R.'s archive. I am grateful to Donald Rainbird, to Ron Green and Tony Millatt of Mersea Museum, Tony Farnham, Stephanie Valentine of Topsail Charters , the Colchester Museum and sailmaker Austin Farrar, whose photos have added to this book; likewise Bob Kemp, for making his father Ted's photograph collection available; Basil Hasler for his wildfowling expertise; Michael Lobb of Radcliffes Gunmakers; Stuart Grimwade of the Ipswich Maritime Trust and Graham Hussey for access to his I.M.T. image collection; photographs from Graham Neilson, Ken and Carol Greenhalgh and Peter Dodds.

Not all the images that have been provided have made it into these pages, but their loan is much appreciated nevertheless.

There are others, too many to name, who have also contributed; to you all, my gratitude. Lastly, but by no means least, my thanks to Brian Webb, who diligently maintains my own collection of photographs.

Jim

When we first heard Jim Lawrence giving a talk about his life in sailing barges from the late forties and fifties at the Marconi Sailing Club we were enthralled by his descriptions of life at sea in a very different age.

We were to meet him by chance at a mutual friend's wake a little later and Margo urged him to commit his memories to paper before they were lost forever and offered to type them. Much to our delight he accepted and together we embarked on a journey into the past.

It was a journey full of colourful characters, humour and tragedy in an age just after the Second World War, when life for ordinary people was so difficult. It was often an age of kindness and sharing between folk who had so little, in comparison with modern times.

By helping Jim to save his memories we feel we have sailed with him on his voyages and have met the amazing array of characters he knew; we hope that within the following pages you will as well.

Margo & Keith Starkey

We've wallowed in the Wallet
Awash with sodden deals,
And slipped from Southend jetty
The Sou'wester at our heels.
Stern winter had his will of us
On black December days,
Our kedge is on the Buxey
And our jib is off the Naze.

R.E.Banyard

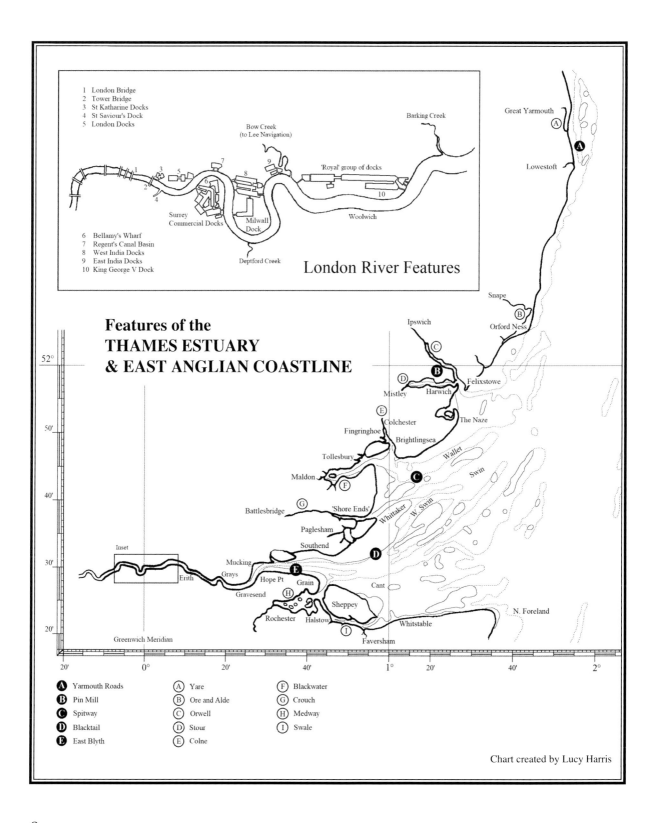

London River Features

1 London Bridge
2 Tower Bridge
3 St Katharine Docks
4 St Saviour's Dock
5 London Docks

6 Bellamy's Wharf
7 Regent's Canal Basin
8 West India Docks
9 East India Docks
10 King George V Dock

Bow Creek
(to Lee Navigation)

Barking Creek

'Royal' group of docks

Surrey
Commercial Docks

Milwall
Dock

Woolwich

Deptford Creek

Features of the
THAMES ESTUARY
& EAST ANGLIAN COASTLINE

Great Yarmouth
Ⓐ

Lowestoft

Snape

Ipswich

Orford Ness

52°

Mistley
Harwich
Felixstowe

Colchester
The Naze

50'

Fingringhoe
Brightlingsea

Waller

Tollesbury

Swin

Maldon

40'

Battlesbridge
'Shore Ends'

Whittaker

W. Swin

Paglesham

Southend

Mucking

30'

Inset

Grays

Erith

Hope Pt
Grain

Cant

Gravesend

Sheppey

N. Foreland

Rochester
Halstow

Whitstable

20'

Greenwich Meridian

Faversham

20'   0°   20'   40'   1°   20'   40'   2°

Ⓐ Yarmouth Roads   Ⓐ Yare   Ⓕ Blackwater
Ⓑ Pin Mill   Ⓑ Ore and Alde Ⓖ Crouch
Ⓒ Spitway   Ⓒ Orwell   Ⓗ Medway
Ⓓ Blacktail   Ⓓ Stour   Ⓘ Swale
Ⓔ East Blyth   Ⓔ Colne

Chart created by Lucy Harris

"Tell me a barge story, Jim."

Possibly the reason why these yarns were ever told was because my grandson Billy was forever saying, "Tell me a barge story, Jim." How many times I had to relate the story of Brownie and his bike I shall never know.

This is the real story of the sailing barge; how she was handled by two men, especially during the winter months when the days were short and the nights long. They were not blue-water sailors with wide open seaways, but made short coastal passages, dodging and sometimes hiding behind the many sandbanks that congest the Thames Estuary and along the East Coast. Summer or winter, night or day, the spritsail barge had to go for as long as weather and tide served. The last band of bargemen, who with determination and love of their craft, kept the remnants of the fleet going long after the time that the barges should have been just memories in the history books. They included the likes of Pat Fisher, Mick Lungley, John Fairbrother, Peter Light, Gordon Hardy, and many more. A special mention must of course go to Bob Roberts, who kept the **Cambria** trading until 1970 and has rightly earned the title of 'the last trading sailorman'.

This is not my life story so much as a social history centred around my working life.

Jim Lawrence
Brightlingsea
2018

Chapter I

London Light

My first boat was our front garden gate when we lived at Colchester Hythe. I got it into my head that it would float, especially if I nailed more wood to it. Carefully unscrewing it from its post, I lugged it a mile to Salary Brook to conduct my sea trials. It floated on its own, but as I climbed aboard it sank six inches to the bottom of the stream. When my dad enquired after the gate I told him that the boys in the other road had pinched it. I was about eleven years old at the time, around 1944.

Half a dozen of us boys were all mad keen to go on the local barges. When we left school, we spent every minute we could around them at Colchester's Hythe Quay, close to my home. Even when skipping school we thought we were training ourselves for our future at work. Careers advice was non-existent, at that time when we all attended the local Wilson Marriage 'Apprehensive' School[1]. It was a bit like that; even the teachers played truant.

We were determined not to let school interfere with our education and we were always down on the Hythe with the sailing barges. We helped to paint and pump them out and we learned to scull boats. With the mast lowered, we could help to poke them further up the Colne to East Mills, and with this experience we felt we were learning our trade for the time we would be ready to leave school and become good barge mates. However our dream was to have our own barge, not easy to achieve for a bunch of school boys. Our enthusiasm and inventiveness came to the rescue via the Colchester Corporation rubbish dump, a goldmine for cash-strapped entrepreneurs in the middle of a war.

At this time, as the allied bombers were penetrating further and further into Germany, they could not carry enough fuel in their regular tanks for the journey there and back. They had to rely on an auxiliary fuel tank under each wing, which was only used for one trip, ending up on the Corporation tip. Each fuel tank was about as

Opposite:
Bargeman and artist Barry Pearce's drawing aboard the sailing barge **Memory** *bound 'London Light', without orders to load, on November 5th., 1956.*

[1] *Wilson Marriage 'Apprehensive' School was a Secondary-Modern in Colchester, later a Comprehensive, hence its nickname.*

big as you could get your arms around and about 10 – 12 feet long, and we saw them as ideal hulls for our boats.

You could buy anything from the dump and so we bought two fuel tanks for half-a-crown each with a receipt of purchase. We were so pleased with them that we made a clandestine visit that night to the dump and pinched six more so that our mates could have some. Eventually the local bobby saw us come ashore and said "Where did you get them tanks from lads, did you pay for them?" We would chorus "Yes sir, our mum paid half-a-crown each for them and keeps the receipt in her purse." We thought that this sounded a plausible story. "Alright," said he, "Bring the receipt up to my house tonight." So off we went to our 'office', which was my best pal and mentor Minnie's dad's former pigeon loft, and found the receipt. That night we went up to the copper's house and knocked timidly on his door. I can picture him now as he came to the door, towering over us with his collar[2] and tie off, and with his service trousers and big boots on. "Come in," he said, and looked at our receipt. "Yes this is all in order; well, behave yourselves and don't fall out of your boats."

A few weeks later he stopped some of our mates and again asked if they had paid for their tanks. They gave the same reply as us and borrowed our receipt to show the copper. He must have read the same receipt at least six times.

Some boys used their tanks as a canoe by cutting a cockpit in them, but unfortunately they were very unstable and tended to roll over. It was quite common to hear of lads getting drowned this way. This was very sad, but did not diminish our determination to build our own 'barge'. We did this by bolting two tanks together effectively making a catamaran, though the word catamaran was not in common use then. This arrangement was very stable, and we had the start of our barge. We were able to fit out well because we could acquire barrage balloon and parachute material from the Corporation dump. This is just what was needed for a young shipping company to get itself started.

We even had navigation lights which we made using a Lyle's Golden Syrup tin, cutting a window in it and some holes for the air to breathe, and simply put a candle inside. Wartime toothpaste came in a tablet form, not much more than hard soap really, wrapped in

2: *Most shirts at this time had separate starched collars attached by a collar stud.*

red or green cellophane, and packed in a tin. We carefully saved the wrapper and stuck it over the cut-out window, giving us port and starboard lights. They worked well but had one fault; with the candles lit the tins got so hot we could not put them out.

We called our barge **Lady Jean**; this was because there was a real barge called **Lady Jean**, and also Minnie's sister was called

Jean, so this seemed a good choice. Very soon after this, Minnie, a year older than me, fell in love with a girl at school called Brenda, and when I went down the Hythe to our barge one evening I saw that our ship's name, **Lady Jean,** was scrubbed out and the name **Lady Brenda** painted in its place. I reacted to this as it is thought very unlucky to change a ship's name. I was determined to have it out with Minnie. When he had finished his tea he came on board and I made my protest. Minnie was

The other **Lady Jean**, almost 50 years later and long retired from cargo carrying, sailing in the 1996 Thames Barge Match.

adamant, stating that he was the skipper and I would have to put up with it. I did not have to wait long as Brenda's mum was one hell of a snob and did not appreciate her daughter going out with Minnie. I could see the reason for this myself; they were just socially apart as Minnie was only in the 'B' stream at school and Brenda was in the 'A' stream; not only that, but she was also a milk monitor.

With Brenda's mum having completely curtailed the romance, the name **Lady Jean** was soon restored to our barge, with Minnie declaring that he had finished with women forever!

Now we had our barge, but we did not want to sail around aimlessly like yachtsmen, we wanted to use it to carry real cargoes. Our opportunity came as a result of war-time rationing causing widespread hunger and a desperate search for alternative sources of food.

At Rowhedge, Mrs. Maudesley had a grocery shop and made homemade jam to sell to her customers without having to take ration coupons from them. We would spend a day picking blackberries. The next day we would load them into our barge. We enjoyed a nice day's sail from Colchester Hythe to Rowhedge where Mrs. Maudesley paid us 4½d per lb. for our fruit. We sailed back to Colchester that evening feeling very pleased with ourselves, having delivered our first freight. This became our regular trade.

These fun days for us as boys seemed to go on for ever, but could not last, particularly as all my friends were older than me. They left school to get jobs in barges as third hands and mates, leaving me languishing at school on my own.

Minnie, my best pal and mentor, was really named Geoff Maynard. He got a job as a mate on a barge called the **Flower of Essex**. Geoff was nicknamed 'Minnie' because we did a school play called Hiawatha. He got the part of Minehaha and the name stuck with him all his life. His skipper rejoiced in the name of Stratford Jack, because he hailed from Stratford, in the East End of London, and that identified him from all the other Jacks.

The **Flower of Essex**.

14

Everyone seemed to have a nickname in those days. One chap I heard about was called Hackney Joe; well, I could work that out. If Stratford Jack came from Stratford, then Hackney Joe must come from Hackney, but that wasn't the case. When I met him I found he was a young boy from Ipswich who simply had a face full of pimples!

One day Minnie said to me, "Why don't you have a day off school tomorrow and come to Maldon. We are on the shipyard there and I want to tar the barge's boat." With great excitement I accepted. I faced a dilemma - I did not want to go on board the barge in short trousers and lose my street credibility. Boys were kept in short trousers until they left school, as long trousers required more clothing coupons than short trousers.I solved the problem by raiding my father's wardrobe and purloining a pair of his grey flannel trousers. With the aid of the bread-knife, I sneaked out to the outside loo and cut the legs so that they would fit me. They were all ragged at the bottom but that did not matter to me; I felt like a real bargeman.

With Minnie, I caught the number 19 bus from Colchester to Maldon for the princely sum of 1/3d. Being hungry boys, our first destination at Maldon was Kathleen's Kitchen where we bought a steaming hot loaf of bread, then off to the butcher to buy a pound of frying steak. You might well ask how we managed to buy a whole pound of frying steak with civilian rationing set to two and a half ounces per week. The music hall joke at the time was that a customer would buy his ration of meat wrapped up in a bus ticket but it would have fallen through the hole in it by the time that he had got home. However, my mate Minnie had a seaman's ration book, which allowed for an abundance of food, and so we had our pound of steak.

We then went next door to the newsagent and brought the Daily Mirror, a very important document, highly acclaimed for helping to win the war. This was largely due to a comic strip, which was greatly enjoyed by the troops fighting in the trenches. I was mostly interested in the adventures of Garth, but Minnie, being older than me, wanted to see what Jane, the striptease artist was taking off.

After these essential preparations we soon arrived at the barge on the shipyard. The cabin was magnificent, with dark polished mahogany panel work, and a large brass lantern hanging over a table. The companionway steps were scrubbed as white as a hound's tooth. My first impressions were of the range of smells: Stockholm tar, black lead, carbolic soap and Mansion polish.

I was to learn that each barge had its own distinctive smell. Later on my wife Pauline could even tell what barge I had been on by the smell adhering to my clothes.

We started work by turning the barge's fourteen foot dinghy over and we gave it a good scrub off. When it had dried we mixed the tar up and heated it over a stove and tarred all over the bottom of the dinghy. When that was done we made the shipwrights a cup of hot tea and cooked our frying steak, before giving the cabin another polish up, for it was always kept spotless.

On the bus home we felt very pleased with our day's work, and Minnie said to me, "Do you fancy a run ashore tonight?" This puzzled me; I thought that being a schoolboy I am always ashore, but I had yet to learn the bargeman's language. However, I had been on the barge all day and felt qualified to say to him that I would like a run ashore. We went to the pictures - my first ever 'run ashore'.

I went back to school and Minnie got his orders to sail 'London light'[3] and load sparta grass[4] for Snodland, above bridges on the River Medway. At school I was thinking of Minnie Maynard, Stratford Jack, and the **Flower of Essex**. These names were like poetry to me - better than any Shakespeare. Snodland sounded so exotic to me then but in my working life I never went there.

In my retirement I took my wife Pauline on a mystery trip to Snodland. It was a little Kentish town about the size of Brightlingsea with a very large paper mill. The sparta grass was used in the production of specialist papers in those days. These days it is also used as a feedstuff for cattle. As I walked along the quay I kicked over one of the iron mooring rings and reflected that it was sixty-three years since Minnie had tied up the **Flower of Essex** there.

[3] *The instruction to the barge's crew regarding the destination for their voyage, London, and the fact that she was to be sailed there empty, or 'light' as it was traditionally known.*
[4] *Sparta grass was used to make 'Baker's Paper', its non-stick properties allowing re-use, providing cost savings over edible rice-based papers, which were single use only.*

Chapter II

First Voyage

At last the time came for me to leave school. It could not come soon enough for me. It was the start of the summer holidays in 1948. They let us school leavers out a bit earlier, saying "We can't teach you anymore" which I thought meant that we knew everything.

I had fixed up to go as third hand in a barge called **Gladys** belonging to Horace Shrubsall. She was known as the **Gladys** of Dover, as opposed to another barge of the same name, which had been built at Harwich. A few years earlier there had been four sailing barges all called **Gladys** - at least there were just two left by then. I ran home from school to collect my gear and say cheerio to mum. She was not too pleased, and had hoped that I would change my mind.

The barge had just unloaded at the Hythe and I knew that she would probably sail the next day. I chucked my gear on deck and called at the foc'sle hatch expecting Doug the mate to be there, but he was not on board. My employment arrangements had all been

The foredeck and foc'sle hatch of the **Gladys** of Dover.

made through him. One pound a week and my grub were the terms that I aspired to, but rarely did I get the pound and not much grub either.

Gingerly I went aft and knocked on the cabin hatch, and called out, "It's Jim Lawrence, skipper, the new third hand," hoping I sounded a bit like an old sea dog rather than the tall gangly just-out-of-school boy that I really was. "Yus," came the reply in a cockney accent, "Git yerself darn the foc'sle and git yerself sorted aht." As I retreated along the deck without having seen the skipper, his voice floated after me, "You've got the starboard bunk." I thought this was rather strange, because the starboard bunk is the senior side, and should have been occupied by the mate.

When I got down the foc'sle I found out why. In pride of place on the starboard side was a huge coal range, leaving a space for my bunk only four feet, ten inches, long! The mate on the other side had a full size bunk. I looked at my miserable little bunk and said to myself, 'Ah well, I can always sleep with my knees curled up.' There was no mattress except for a mat. It was a sort of mat that grandads made with bits of wool pulled through a sack with a pricker. I think it was called a thrum mat.

This was to be my mattress and it looked as if it had not had a shake since it had been a mat.

My own gear that I had brought on board included an army overcoat; this to be my eiderdown if it was cold in bed, or my oilskins if it was wet on deck. It was the devil's own job to dry the coat once it had got saturated and the skipper, fed up with seeing it hanging in the rigging, simply chucked it overboard. I also had two blankets, plus a kitbag with my spare clothes in, which would also serve as a pillow. Besides this sparse collection, I had a Quality Street sweet tin full of buns that my mother had cooked for me; half were currant buns, and half were plain currant buns, because when mum ran out of currants, which were rationed, she had to make plain currant buns. The mate ate these whilst I was seasick. When I eventually turned in on that first night, I noticed carved in the beam above my head - CERT' TO ACCOM' ONE SEAMAN - I had made it at last!

I must have slept very soundly for the next thing I heard was noises on deck; I rushed up and discovered that Doug the mate was already letting go our lines for'ard whilst the skipper attended to those aft and the tug was waiting to tow us away down the River Colne from Colchester. This was my first trip as a real bargeman and we were bound 'London light'.

As we got down the river I noticed that Doug and the skipper were not talking to each other but Doug knew what to do and so I took my orders from him. Between us we got the sails set and the tug let us go at the Iron Bridge, Alresford, the usual place to tow to. As we tacked out of the Colne it was blowing quite hard and there were two or three barges laying windbound, but we continued past them. I can picture our barge now, it was marvellous, as she swooped up and down on the waves like a big whale with spray cascading over her deck. Doug said to me, "Alright?" and I grinned back, "It's smashing." He laughed and said, "It won't be like this much longer."

As that lovely August day wore on the sky got darker, the wind fresher, and the barge heeled more and more. We had to reduce her canvas, and I noticed that we were a long way from land with only a low coastline showing on the horizon. It was here that we dropped anchor; it seemed to me a very strange place to stop as we seemed to be miles from the shore. It was a place called the West Buxey. I learned that it was a good sheltered place, although the land was low and gave little protection, but the tides were slack with shallow water and we were ready for a slant to London.

We lay there for three days, rolling and tumbling about. I felt ill but could not be sick and had eaten nothing. The skipper had his wife aboard and she came to see me. "Nobby's getting worried about you, he thinks you should drink a glass of seawater and make yourself sick." Well, I did not have to have a glass of seawater to make myself sick then, just mere mention of it was enough to make me vomit. I was sick over the side and then went below to eat the barge out of house and home until, that is, the mate put the brakes on.

When we reached London, Grays actually, I went ashore and found that I was walking like a drunk. After so many days on board, a heaving deck seemed normal, but dry land seemed to be coming up to meet me. This phenomenon soon wore off, but I will never forget it.

At Grays I became aware of what the great name of E. J. & W. Goldsmith had once meant to the barging world. It had been the largest fleet of all, and when they ordered new barges it was for 20 vessels at a time. Now the remnants of that once great fleet were laid at anchor with no work in the offing. The loyal crews were hoping for the company fortunes to pick up, but they never did for the barge work. Shortly afterwards most of their fleet was sold off to The London and Rochester Trading Company. Many of them never sailed again.

As a young boy of 15 this made me very sad, but optimism would not allow me to think of this as what the future might hold.

Grays waterfront was just how Dickens would have seen it, thirty or forty barges laying at their anchors with barge boats going to and from the ancient stone causeway. Ashore stood the famous 'Theobald Arms', with weatherboarded cottages lining the lower part of the high street. This has all now been redeveloped but somehow the 'Theobald Arms' has survived.

After three days we received our orders to go to the Millwall dock, where the central granary was located, to load wheat. We loaded up and headed for Felixstowe.

As third hands, the skippers would often have fun at our expense. The war had only just finished; there were no lighted buoys in the Swin and our only aids to navigation was the compass, the lead line and the skippers' own intimate knowledge of the surrounding sand banks. The lead line was a 7lb weight with a rope attached, marked out every fathom to measure the depth of water. For example if the depth was two and half fathoms, you would call out "AND a half two." or "LESS a quarter two.", for one and three quarter fathoms.

With the water running along the deck and the noise of the wind, it was difficult to be heard on a windy night. At the bottom of the lead there was a hole into which we would insert some carbolic soap to bring up a sample of the seabed. This was a great aid to navigation because the Admiralty chart would show the composition of the seabed in different places; e.g. shell, shingle, mud and sand. An experienced skipper would know this information by heart, and even in the dark would know exactly where he was.

Gladys at the Southend Corporation Jetty. She was built by Felton at Sandwich in 1900.

My skipper, Nobby (Nobby Norman), had me heaving the lead all night, my hands were red raw and I was soaked to the skin as I was shouting out soundings. Every now and again he would shout, "What's the bottom like boy?" and I would shout back, "Sharp sand and shingle, skip." "That's fine," he would shout back, "Keep the lead going." As we neared shallow water I got more tense; if the barge went ashore it was bound to be my fault. As I shouted as loud as I could, "AND a half one." he asked me what was the bottom like. "Soft mud." I replied. "You sure?" he cried, "It should be shingle - lick it boy, lick it!" So I licked it, and said, "Just soft mud, skip." He replied, "Yeah I thought so, we are just going over the sewage outfall."

As third hand of the **Gladys** I hated to be called cook, because I wanted to be respected as the third hand. The skipper's comments, like, "Put plenty of salt in those spuds boy; perhaps they will cry their eyes out!" or "Boy couldn't cook hot water without burning it!" did nothing to improve my confidence.

After we had moored up at Felixstowe the skipper gave Doug a pound note as a sub and cleared off ashore, leaving Doug and I to see the barge unloaded. He was gone for three days and after the second day we were out of grub. On the third day we both decided to leave, but I must hand it to Doug that he would not desert and intended to stay until Nobby returned and he could hand the responsibility over properly.

We both sat down in the foc'sle very hungry, and I said to Doug, "Would you like me to make you a cake?" Doug glared at me and swore; "What with?" I replied that there was some flour in the cupboard, and with this I mixed up a gooey mess with some water and popped it into the oven. We were so hungry that we only left it in for twenty minutes and it was barely warm. I spread a spoonful of jam over the mess and that is how we ate it.

A couple of hours later, Doug sprung into action and exclaimed, "Come on, we are going to break into Nobby's cabin." He prised open the skylight and threaded me down into the cabin below. I was quite thin then and we had a sumptuous feast from Nobby's grub locker. We replaced the skylight lid so that it would not show that it had been tampered with. On Nobby's return we both said that we were off, leaving the **Gladys**. He did not seem at all perturbed that he was losing such a good mate in Doug and shoved a few pound notes into his hand, promising to send on the rest, which Doug doubted. For my part, I had found the Gladys an unhappy ship under Nobby's command and was glad to be gone. I reviewed my first voyage and decided that I was ready to try for a job as a mate.

The **Gladys** was eventually wrecked, and ended up on Deadman's Island, a huge expanse of saltings in the Medway. Many years later I sailed to her with my wife Pauline on our bawley, the **Saxonia**, since Deadman's Island can only be reached by boat. The **Gladys** was laying there with her back broken and falling to pieces. I took a piece of wood from her which had been part of my bunk, and I thought that I would fit it into my fireplace at home as a memento.

Gladys wrecked near the Grain Spit in 1960. She was moved to Shepherd's Creek where her decaying hulk slowly returns to nature on Deadman's Island.

Fifty years after she was abandoned on Deadman's Island, **Gladys** continues to decay, but slowly.

Pauline asked me why it was called Deadman's Island, and I had to confess to her that this was where they buried some of the plague victims in the 1600s. She spent the next three days gargling with TCP!

Nobby, before going as skipper of the **Gladys** had, during the war, been skipper of a steel barge named **Ailsa**. She struck a mine in the Whitaker Channel on the 13th January 1943 and was blown to bits. Nobby, the mate and the dog were all blown clear and were picked up by a barge following them, skippered by a Maldon bargeman named Arthur Keeble. It is strange but only a coincidence that Arthur was going to be my next skipper in a barge called the **Falconet**.

Chapter III

Arthur Keeble

My opportunity came with a barge called **Falconet** at Colchester that needed a new mate, as the previous mate was leaving to get married and to work ashore. The skipper was a Maldon man named Arthur Keeble, who had known me since I was at school. He agreed to give me the job, even though I was fifteen at the time and he was in his sixties. As a young man, Arthur had been in the stack work. In those days there were more horses in London than motorcars today. The local farmers used to send all the straw and hay to London for the horse bedding and feed, and bring all the horse muck back to Essex for the fields. This sounds very environmentally friendly but you can have too much of a good thing. In 1890 Parliament was recalled to discuss the health hazards in London, which was fast disappearing under a tide of horse manure.

A stackie, the Maldon **Eva Annie**, turns up the London River; the mate keeps watch atop the stack, telling the skipper when to tack, whilst the barge dog keeps watch to windward!

Arthur's job as a stackie was to load the stacks of hay fourteen feet high on the deck. Once the barge was under way, the mate would have to be on top of the stack to shout information to the skipper as he had great difficulty in seeing where he was going. The skipper would hold a straight course by observing the wake of the barge. When the skipper put the tiller over to tack it gave him a brief chance to peer along the side of the stack to see where he was going. In the picture you can see that the dog is looking down the windward side of the stack. When people ask if it is true that these barges could be sailed by two men and a dog, you would say yes, but that it had to be bloody good dog!.

They would tack up the Thames to the Lower Pool of London, below Tower Bridge, where they would make a slot in the haystack so the mast could be lowered to get under the fixed bridges. It was a hard old job, which was all over by the time I started my barging career.

In 1911 Arthur had been skipper in a barge called **Pride of Essex**. On the 14th December that year the stack caught fire and she burnt out. This was not many days before Christmas, and since Arthur was without a barge, they sent him to Faversham to pick up a barge called **Charles & Isabella**, loaded with ragstone to be brought back to Maldon.

The weather forecasting was very poor in those days, and Arthur set sail for Maldon and encountered a severe gale. This bad weather had not been forecast and caused much damage ashore as well as at sea. **Charles & Isabella** was blown onto the Gunfleet sands, where she was wrecked. Arthur had to burn his bedding to attract attention, and when the tide came up he and his mate had to climb the rigging as the deck was submerged.

Anchored in the Pool of London, a stack barge would lower her gear for the passage above bridges, either towed by a tug, or setting 'bridge sails' when the wind serves. **Eva Annie** is probably to discharge at a wharf in the Pool as there is no sign of her planning to lower down.

25

His burning bedding was seen by the Coastguard at Walton, who sent out a lifeboat called the **James Stephens**[5], which was powered by sail and oars, to rescue Arthur and his mate. 1,2,3,4

As an open boat, I often wondered about the discomfort that Arthur and his mate endured in their journey ashore in the lifeboat, covered only in an old piece of canvas and shivering from hours of hanging from the rigging. I could not help reflecting on the Christmas the Keeble family would have had, since Arthur had lost two barges in less than a week - one on the 14th December and one on the 20th. As he said to me years later, "Burnt out and washed out all in one week, Jim." Although he made light of it, it could not have been so laughable at the time.

These events were all ancient history by 1948 when Arthur and I loaded English wheat at Colchester Hythe to go up to Vauxhall, through eleven bridges on the Thames.

When leaving the Colne, a loaded barge would sometimes be hard-headed in a strong easterly; the mizzen stowed, and three cloths of the mainsail brailed up, would make her steering lighter. Rarely was the topsail lowered, usually for a sharp squall. **Falconet** did not carry davits, so the boat was towed on two large bass painters.

Falconet laden, leaves the Colne in a smart easterly breeze.

[5] The **James Stephens** lifeboat has now, over one hundred years later, been rebuilt with a Heritage Lottery Fund grant, and is moored in Titchmarsh Marina, Essex, available to charter.

We arrived at a place known as the Mud Hole just outside of St. Katherine Docks. It was called the Mud Hole because the mud that was dredged from there was suitable for making bricks.

After anchoring and lowering the mast in preparation for our journey under the eleven bridges to Vauxhall, we were towed up the river by tug to our destination. On the quay at Vauxhall we had to raise our mast again in order to remove the hatches and unload our cargo.

By the time we had completed this, a thick London smog had descended and visibility was reduced to a few yards. The smog was so thick that you could even taste it[6].

Once we were unloaded Arthur was anxious to get down the river again, but said that nothing would be working in those conditions. With the typical independence and resourcefulness of a bargeman, he decided that we would come out on the tide and 'drudge' down the river. 'Drudging' was used in strongly flowing tidal waters and involved lowering the anchor just enough to drag along the bottom, so that the barge with the mast lowered would travel backwards with the skipper steering the vessel in reverse. The mate meanwhile would stay in the bows, and check that the anchor had not fouled anything and was allowing the barge to move in a controlled way. Arthur did a great job and I was very impressed with the way he steered the barge under each bridge. All went well until we got under London Bridge, where we stopped dead when the anchor fouled on an underwater object. I could not heave the anchor up because it was stuck fast against the strongly ebbing tide.

Arthur Keeble, aged 26, aboard the **Pride of Essex**, c.1910.

[6:] *In those days smoke combined with fog to create a toxic yellow murk called smog, which killed three thousand Londoners every year before the Clean Air Act was brought in in 1956.*

The abutments of the bridge and the barge itself caused the water to flow faster around us, making the barge roll and pitch. It required the combined efforts of both Arthur and I to haul the anchor up, when we discovered that it was hooked onto a large electric cable, as big as you could get your hands round. We did not know if it was alive or

A tiller-steered barge, gear lowered down, drudges, stern first, under the bascules of Tower Bridge.

not, but we had to get a slip rope round it so that we could free the anchor. Arthur warned me to keep my hands well clear when releasing the slip rope as it would have stretched to twice its usual length under this abnormal load. I am glad that I heeded his advice since it whipped and thrashed about alarmingly when I released it and could have caused a serious injury. We negotiated Tower Bridge successfully, and once anchored back at the Mud Hole we hoisted our mast up again, still surrounded by the dense smog. We were the only boat on the river to have moved that day. As we sat down to have our tea that evening I reflected that for a man in his sixties and a fifteen year old boy we hadn't done a bad day's work.

Arthur was a lovely bloke to get on with; the only contention we had was the amount of food I ate. This may have been because Arthur was stout and I was tall and like a bean pole, with the healthy appetite of a teenager. Arthur reckoned I used to "eat on purpose", and if I cut myself an extra slice of bread he would say, "Baker don't call, Jim!" To get round this problem I used to hide an extra loaf of bread in a hidden shelf in my bunk, together with a tin of Lyle's Golden Syrup. Although I was paying for my own grub, he used to get upset because I was always hungry and he seemed to require so little.

Another barge skipper, Bill 'Coddy' Polly of **Beric**, once had thirteen loaves of bread in his cupboard. He simply bought a fresh

Colchester, a port since Roman times, Owen Parry's oil mill on the Hythe, on an early postcard.

loaf every time he went ashore, but so that he ate the old bread first he cut the date of the purchase through the crust in roman numerals with a razor blade. This meant that he was always eating old bread.

We were laying windbound once at Shore Ends with another barge named **Ethel Ada**. This was the Shrubsall **Ethel Ada**, built at Ipswich. By evening the weather had turned fine, and Arthur decided to scull down to the other barge and have a yarn with her skipper. The mate on the other barge was my old friend Minnie Maynard, so he sculled up to our barge to have a yarn with me. He was also kept hungry by his skipper, and asked me if I had any grub. "Yeah," I said, "I've got a loaf of bread here that Arthur don't know about." So we got the bread out and smeared the syrup on it for a great feast. It was all running down our chops - we were having a lovely time.

We were so engrossed we did not notice the time until a bump alongside announced the imminent return of Arthur. "Quick," I said, "Get this bread and syrup back into my bunk before Arthur sees it." We had cleared the table and wiped it down by the time Arthur arrived, and were just sitting yarning. I thought I had got away with it until I turned in that night, and discovered that in his haste Minnie had not put the lid back on the syrup tin properly, leaving a awful sticky mess in my bunk. The next morning when I awoke it looked as if I was wearing socks because all the blanket fluff had stuck to my feet.

Sometimes of course, through laying windbound or held up with fog, you would actually run out of grub, or get very low in the grub locker. This happened on the **Raybel** once, and when the hungry mate said, "Have we got anything for breakfast?" Albie Webb, the skipper, replied, "Well, if we had some eggs we could have some eggs and bacon, if we had some bacon!"

It was customary on all barges that when turning in for the night you would turn the cabin lamp down low, but just aglim. This was in case you had to turn out in the night to deal with any emergency. Also, if the skipper was thinking of making a very early start he would probably turn out several times in the night to check if the weather was remaining in a settled state. I found it very amusing when Arthur turned out because he wore immaculate white long johns complete with a long-sleeved vest. Us young 'uns thought this very old-fashioned, and Arthur, being a bit portly, would add his thick leather belt to his attire together with his cap before going on deck.

Once he had retired again to his bunk I knew if we were going to muster, as great clouds of smoke would billow from his bunk as he lit his pipe, then after a short time he would call, "Put the kettle on, Jim."

Besides the coal range in the foc'sle, there was also in the cabin aft, an open fire contained in an ornate fire place, with fire bars in the front to hold the coals in. On these bars would be a trivet on which stood a huge black kettle full of near-boiling water. This kettle would happily sing away all day with occasional bouts of steam coming out of the spout. If the skipper said, "Make a cuppa tea boy," you would simply put your foot out and push the trivet closer to the heat. By the time that you got the cups and teapot out the kettle would be boiling. This was the best cup of tea ever, as it had a distinct smoky taste.

In the summertime when you did not need a fire, you would have a thin tin kettle. This would simply be boiled on the primus stove or sometimes a stick fire in the hearth would be employed. The tin kettle, though allowed to go black on the

Owen Parry's oil mill is seen in the middle distance in this view of Colchester Hythe, their little steam barge **Gem** just up-river of the mill.

31

Owen Parry's **Vera** at Cochester Hythe, a 'stack' of linseed oil barrels fill her deck space and, no doubt, her cargo space below.

bottom and sides, would be brightly polished on the top, handle and spout with Brasso.

I loved to paint the barge, but the owner was miserly about the amount of paint we could use I remember one occasion we had a gallon tin of lovely golden brown paint which I was going to use to paint the inside rails. We were laying at Colchester; I got up early and made a start. At about 9am, Arthur arrived off the bus carrying a brown paper carrier bag.

"I see you've made an early start, Jim," he exclaimed; "I told mother that you were giving the ol' girl a coat of paint and so she dug out these rags for you to wipe the odd spots up, there's bound to be a few." He came down the ladder onto the deck and went aft, but did not go down the cabin and left the carrier bag next to the hatch. He then went ashore again and said that he would not be long but he was going to the office to see if we had any new orders.

I resumed my painting, and a few minutes later, had a disaster and tipped the can of paint over. Panicking because our precious paint was being wasted I hurriedly scooped what I could back into the tin as best I could with the three inch brush.

Both sides of the River Colne at Colchester Hythe lined with sailing barges, a big ketch barge on the left. Owen Parry's **King** is unloading timber for Groom, Daniels & Co.'s timber yard to the east of the river.

I didn't do a bad job but there was just one big stain left on the deck. Thank God for those rags, I thought, and went aft to fetch them. Grabbing a handful of them, I got most of it up and then went down the foc'sle to get some paraffin oil. Pouring this on the deck I used more rags to finally clean the deck so that no paint spill could be seen. I topped the paint tin up with some paraffin oil and stirred it in so that Arthur would not realise that I had spilt any. After I had chucked the soiled rags overboard to complete my cleaning up, I realised that they were laying on the top of the mud because the tide was out. I could not leave them there in full view, so using the boat hook, the rags were pushed two feet under the mud.

By the time Arthur returned I was painting again, albeit with thinned paint, but it did not show too much. Arthur surveyed my work and then said, "If you want any of those rags to wipe up Jim, you'll find them in the carrier bag under my clean underpants and vest."

Despite the destruction of his underwear, Arthur and I got on very well, and he was always willing to teach me more about my craft.

We were sailing down the Swin heading for East Mills, and Arthur said to save our tides and reach our destination we would have to sail through the night. "Light the lamps, Jim." he said, so I went down the foc'sle where the large navigation lamps were kept. I lit them on a low level to allow them to warm up before struggling on deck with them, almost too heavy for a fifteen year old to carry. If I had lit them on deck in such cold weather the glass would have cracked. Once the lamps were shipped Arthur said, "Time for you to try a bit of celestial navigation." This meant that I was going to have a steer. With Arthur's vast experience of the area he relied only on a compass and stars at night. "Jim, you see that big star up there, keep that on the end of the crosstree." I said, "Olright." because by now I was fairly confident with my steering although I had never done this at night. Arthur said, "I'm just going below for a while." and left me to it. I really felt a big man now, as we were deep-loaded and the water was sloshing along both decks.

After an hour or so there was no sign of Arthur and I suspected that he had fallen asleep sitting on his locker. By this time the star was no longer at the end of the crosstrees; the concentration of a fifteen year old is difficult to maintain for over an hour. Rather concerned I might run the barge ashore, I went and knocked on the hatch and called timidly down, "Arthur, I think that we have passed that one; can you find me another?"

Of course all of us young lads wanted to show that we were good mates to our skippers, and our duties were very varied. Sailing up to London, the wind was invariably from the southwest and we

Sailing barges **Imperial** and **Paglesham**; Groom, Daniels & Co.'s timber yard in the background.

would have to tack out of the Colne. I would be handling the sails, and raising and lowering leeboards each time we tacked, but I also had to prepare dinner. I lit the coal range and got a duff on (suet pudding). However, we did not use a basin, as ashore, but used a cloth tied up with a special piece of white string. If you lost your piece of white string you would have to tie it up with a piece of spunyarn, and then the tar would come out of the spunyarn and into the pudding.

As well as the duff I would be cooking a leg of lamb in the oven and preparing the greens. Every time the skipper yelled down "'BOUT OH" it would mean it was time to tack again. I would run on deck, tend to the sails, raise and lower the leeboards before dashing below to put more coal on the fire. Of course the skipper would swear at you if you let the duff go off the boil because he reckoned that it would "mess it up". This meant that I would have to put a little coal on at a time to keep the fire bright rather than stoking it high in one go. If you could manage all these things simultaneously, you were doing quite well. At dinner time I would bring all the food aft and set it up on the table in the cabin. When I went to tell the skipper it was ready he would say, "'Ere, take the wheel, Jim", and he would go below for his grub and light his pipe. Later he would return and say, "Alright boy, you can go and get yours now;" of course by that time the food was cold.

This may seem very hard but it was the normal pattern in a sailing barge with only two crew, and the skipper always took precedence. Some of Arthur's ideas seem very quaint now; if you wore four pairs of underpants you were being sensible, but if you wore a pair of gloves you were being a sissy.

Chapter IV

Working for Marriages

The time came for Arthur to retire, and I shipped into a barge called the **Leofleda** as mate which was owned by Marriages. It was much the same sort of work, bringing wheat down from London to Marriages Mill at Colchester and taking flour back to London. The wheat was always shot in loose, but the flour was loaded in bags. A bag of flour would weigh one and a quarter hundredweight, which was 140 pounds, and we would load sixteen hundred of these bags, giving us one hundred tons of freight. The skipper, Charlie Sheldrake, and I would have to load these ourselves; the bags would come down a chute into the open hatchway, and we would stow them very carefully below. Fully loaded, we would sail up to Winchester Wharf in London, just through London Bridge, and unload the flour. Marriages would then have another freight of wheat for us to take back to Colchester East Mills. Before we could go up to the Mill we had to lower our mast because we had to negotiate four bridges and one and half miles of river to reach the unloading berth.

W. & H. Marriage & Sons, East Mills, Colchester, a tortuous destination for sailing barges, laden or light.

We could not sail and so we had to poke up to the mill using setting booms, which on the Broads are called quants. Although **Leofleda** was built for the East Mills work, she was in fact one of the most awkward barges to go there. Nine hatches on the forward part of her main hold had to be turned upside down to allow the gear to be laid as low as possible. A man called a huffler was taken on to help us; he was usually a retired bargeman. On one occasion we had a huffler named Brownie and we had to go up on the night tide. It was as black as the ace of

Prior's **Mayland**, George Bowles, skipper, and his mate, with two hufflers on board, 'starting up' the long poke to East Mills. The ship laying at Groom, Daniels & Co.'s timber yard is the **Orion** of Hansweert, one of the many Dutch coasters part-financed by the Dutch Government, and in direct competition with the sailing barges.

spades with no moon. We gathered on the deck of the barge at 1.00 a.m., just as the tide was starting to make. It was essential to get up the river before the tide was too high or else we would not pass under the bridges. We would leave as soon as we were afloat, with just the rudder trailing the ground.

Just as we were about to leave Charlie asked Brownie if he wanted a cuppa. "'Ere boy," said Brownie to me, "Go ashore and bring my bike aboard." I distinctly remember bringing the bike aboard before we came afloat whilst the skipper and huffler were having their tea below. "Come on, we're afloat," I shouted down to them and they came tumbling up on deck. We had an uneventful trip up to the mill in pitch darkness, and Brownie helped us heave the mast up ready for the grain to be sucked out of the hold. It was at this point that Brownie said, "'Ere boy, where did you put my bike?" Perplexed, I replied, "It must be

Dawn poking up to the Mill, about to pass under the Hythe road bridge. When she is lowered down as flat as possible, a barge has an air draft of about 5'. When fully rigged, she has an air draft of around 90'.

'ere somewhere, I remember putting it aboard." It was nowhere to be seen, and he gave me a ding around the lughole, saying, "You've left it back at the Hythe boy, now I will have to go all the way back to fetch it." He then walked off very grumpy and I turned in thinking I was convinced that I had put the bike aboard. The riddle was solved when we got up the next morning in daylight and could see it hoved up on the mast, hanging on the crosstrees.

East Mills, before the grain sucker was installed; note the barge behind has a gin wheel rigged for lifting out cargo. Both barges are tiller steered, and the background craft has a lug-rigged mizzen.

Just through East Bridge, heaving up the **Leofleda**'s gear to give access to her hatcheways. Note the crews from other barges assisting on the windlass handles. The deep-loaded barge ahead of **Leofleda** is the **Dawn**, the barge to starboard (half-unloaded) is the **British Empire**.

Above right: Marriage's **Leofleda**, deep laden, runs before the breeze, her boat towing astern.

I never felt really settled in this job, and looked for another opportunity. The previous mate had left the **Leofleda** having had an argument at the Mill, and his parting words were, "stow your own *?!@$# dumpling dust, I'm off!"

Arthur Rook, the new skipper of the **Falconet**, asked me, "How about coming back to your old barge, Jim?" I jumped at the chance because Arthur Rook trusted me to get on with the work and not stand over me checking everything. I would work like hell to beat Arthur on any job but I never could. Arthur would ask me to get the barge ready to sail whilst he would do the washing up, giving me a chance to hone my sailing skills. It took twenty minutes to get the barge ready to sail, but Arthur only ten minutes to wash up! I rushed around setting the sails, lowering the leeboards and heaving the anchor up.

Arthur could tell how far I had got by the noises on the deck, and just as the anchor was breaking out of the ground he would arrive

Arthur Rook - my second skipper, when in the **Falconet**.

on deck with his pipe in his mouth and say, "Alright boy, I've got her now," as he took charge of the wheel. However, his trust in me strengthened my self-confidence, culminating one day as we lay at Hope Point in a gale of wind. Arthur said, "I don't like being here- if we drag our anchor we will finish up on the sea wall."

I could see the old boy was worried, and that we wouldn't get any sleep that night, so I suggested, "It's flood tide Arthur; with a bit of flood under our bow and some sail on we can get her off of here." Arthur sprung into action and ordered me to go light the lamps. We had to struggle to get the thirty fathoms of chain in against the gale of wind, but if we had stayed, the ebb tide would have left us in a dangerous position. Once under weigh we shot across the river to the Lower Hope, which is a large expanse of anchorage, and by three in the morning we were anchored again with thirty fathoms of chain out once more.

We staggered below after our exertions and Arthur exclaimed, "Shall we have some supper, boy?" "Yeah," I replied, "we have got some bubble and squeak left." Relaxing after our meal, Arthur said to me unexpectedly, "This job has made a man of you, Jim, hasn't it." "What do you mean Arthur?" "Well," says he, "So many skippers have got bits of boys for mates, but you really showed that you knew what to do earlier. I am going to speak to the guv'nor when we get back."

He kept his word and I was duly summoned into the guv'nor's office. "Arthur is very pleased with you, Jim, and we want you to stay with the firm and become one of our skippers by the time that you are twenty-one." Well I thought, that was marvellous, because I had never had a compliment paid to me before in my life. Being Arthur's mate was a very pleasant experience because he built up my confidence, and as he was single I would sometimes take him home to dinner.

Next to us lived Mrs Hughes, a little widow lady, and Arthur took a fancy to her. Blow me, he had only taken her out twice and they decided to get married. This made him decide to retire and so **Falconet** was laid up again without a skipper.

Josh Francis - of
barge owners
Francis & Gilders.

It was about this time my dad died, and with three of us still at home I had to be the main breadwinner. This would mean finding a better paid job and the end of my barging career. I duly wrote to Shell, who were having a tanker built at Middlesborough. They replied that when they were recruiting crew they would get in touch with me.

Josh Francis, owner of the firm, sent down for me and asked, "What are you going to do, Jim?" He knew my situation and said that he did not blame me for seeking better paid employment elsewhere to support my family. However, he asked, "Can you help me out for just a fortnight?" I replied, "I will if I can as I have not heard from Shell yet." "Well," he went on, "the mate of the **George Smeed** having jammed his thumb in the windlass, is going to be off for two weeks. Bert Oxley, the skipper, needs a mate in the meantime." She was a bigger barge and therefore a big earner as we were paid by the share for each voyage and not a weekly wage. Bert had a reputation for pushing on hard, and I had an opportunity to earn more money. I therefore agreed to be Bert's mate for the next fortnight.

Bertie Oswald Byford Oxley was a tough old bird, having sailed around the world twice in square-riggers as a young man, but had turned to barging when he got married so that he could have more 'home time'.

I introduced myself to Bert at Pin Mill, and at five the next morning we shoved off from the hard. It was an absolute flat calm, and we drove (drifted) down the river on the ebb and out of the Harbour. We picked up a few light airs, and the flood tide took us up the Wallet. With so much tide and so little wind we were taken past the Spitway, where we normally crossed to get into the Swin; instead we were sent up the Rays'n Channel across to the Shore Ends. When the ebb tide came down Bert did not anchor as most skippers would have done, but drove on down the Whitaker and across into the Swin, where the next flood tide took us up towards Southend. I had been doing most of the steering up until then, but when we picked up a fresh southwesterly, Bert took the wheel and I stood by the tops'l halliard because of the strength of the wind. We got to the East Blyth at high water and Bert decided that we should

The '100 ton' **George Smeed** was built by Smeed Dean in 1882 to carry c.40,000 bricks from their Murston, Kent, brickworks to London. Smeed Dean rebuilt her in 1922 as a 'rose-upon' with flared sides, thus she was 17' wide on the bottom and 20' wide at the deck, increasing her cargo capacity to 150 tons. Seen here sailing up Ipswich Dock to discharge at Cranfield's mill, after her rebuild.

anchor there. We had been underway for twenty-three hours continuously just to get from Pin Mill to Southend.

This was typical of Bert, he would never miss an opportunity to press on if he could, and I started to earn more money. At the end of the fortnight I went to see Josh Francis, the owner, who asked me how I was getting on with Bert. I was very pleased to reply, "Great skipper." "He is very pleased with you," said Josh, "and would like you to stay with him. The other mate is not coming back."[11,12]

Yippee! This took me completely by surprise, and it meant that with the extra money I could stay with barging, my first love, rather than be forced to ship on a tanker with Shell.

This was the start of a fruitful time for me in the **George Smeed** with Bert, who was not only an enormously experienced seaman but also a talented raconteur with a fund of stories about his times in the square-riggers.

One of my favourites concerned the medicines carried by these vessels to tend to the ailments of the crew on long sea voyages. No doctor was carried on board of course, so the skipper would go ashore before the start of the voyage to stock up the medicine chest. At the apothecary's he topped up with the medicines that he was short of, but of course the Latin names meant nothing to him at all. He got around this by labeling the jars in numerical order, eg: No.1 for headaches, No.2 for sore throats etc.

One of his crew went aft to him towards the end of one voyage complaining that he did not feel very well. The skipper listened to his symptoms and decided that he needed some of No.7. However when he opened the medicine chest he found that all of No. 7 had been used, so he gave him a drop of No. 3 and a drop of No.4 instead.

Bert had been born in 1884, which incidentally was two years after the **George Smeed** had been built. He was one of the best skippers that I ever sailed with, and in the time I was with him he enhanced my career so much, because he taught me so many things.

The **George Smeed** was no great shakes as a flier, but under Bert's command she certainly had her moments. One time we had just

The **George Smeed** loaded with 30 standards of timber.

unloaded timber onto the Southend Corporation Jetty, and our orders were to return light to Osea Island to load timber from a ship anchored off there. **George Smeed** could load around 30 standards of timber with a stack on the hatches. Although a 'standard' was cubic measure, it averaged about two and a half tons in weight. The stack meant we had to have the foresail reefed up, with wire forehorse, and the mainsail likewise, with a wire mainhorse going over the stack. Chains and timbers secured the stack. We lost the use of the mast-case winches; these were usually unshipped to avoid interfering with the stow, and would be placed in the empty space inside the coaming of the forehatch. A spider band would be rigged on the mast for cleats. We also lost the use of the rigging cleats and had to lash a batten across the rigging for the peak brails, etc., to be made fast to.

The wind was blowing about Force 7 from the southwest. Luckily we were laying on the lee side of the jetty, otherwise we would not have been able to fetch off. Bert stepped on board about two hours before high water; the skipper of the S.B. **Ashingdon** was on the jetty to tend our big bass rope which we set up on the fore horse as a spring. With full mainsail, topsail and foresail she first set back on the spring, then leapt forward. We needed a good offing as the then gasworks jetty was just under our lee. Once clear Bert shouted, "Give me a hand to bear away," and we ran down along the shore, very close in it seemed to me. The Mulberry Harbour wreck appeared to be very far to the south. There was no boom defence there at this time. The wartime one had been demolished, and the present one was constructed later during the Cold War with Russia. Bert held her in close to the shore over the Ridge and across the Raysand channel, holding right tight up to Sales Point.

Once in the Blackwater with the tide hard away, all we could do was shoot up head to wind and give her the anchor with 25 fathoms of chain. I ran below and checked the time. "Bert," I said, "We've been three hours!" Bert grinned and said, "I doubt if you will ever do that again, Jim." I haven't and I won't. What a bloke! My time with Bert came to an abrupt end six months later at the Surrey Docks. We were going through the bridge hole where they had swung the bridge open for us. We heaved about the dock by attaching fifty fathoms of dolly line forward to anything convenient ashore, like a bollard. The dolly winch would heave you up to this, and then the mate would take a turn around something else and the process would be repeated, until you got to your destination

As we were heaving through the bridge hole, a tug coming the other way hit our bow and started the barge moving backward. Bert was unable to let go of the handle of the winch in time as it rotated out of control and smashed his right arm. He lay on the deck in considerable pain whilst I rushed to try and board the barge again as it drifted, and the tug continued on its way oblivious to the consequences of their actions. To them it was just a game.

I caught the barge up and managed to moor it with a single line, and then got Bert up to the Greenwich Hospital to be sorted out. When I returned to the barge, I knew that I had to get round into the Canada Dock ready for loading the next morning. I retrieved the dolly wire which had pulled off the winch, fixed only on the shore and trailing in the water. I re-installed it on the winch and started to heave the barge through the bridge hole. It was dark by the time I went into the bridgeman's hut to request him to swing the bridge open. I also asked him the name of the tug that had gone through at quarter to seven that evening, but he denied that any tug had been there. He had come on duty at eight p.m., and the previous shift had wiped the chalk board which showed ship movements clean, to hide the evidence. They had closed ranks to protect one of their own so that Bert could never claim compensation.

"Send one over…" A set of timber being handled aboard ship.

A timber hook – a vicious weapon, but used to handle cargo.

I spent the rest of the night getting the barge round to the timber ship from which we were due to load our cargo. The next day our cargo was loaded and in the evening I went to the hospital to see how Bert was getting on. Bert said that with his arm broken in several places it was not possible for him to return to the barge. He had talked to the guv'nor on the telephone and recommended that I should be promoted to skipper; this was just one month after my eighteenth birthday. The guv'nor had agreed. I was overjoyed with the news, but had very mixed feeling because of the injuries to Bert. The faith and trust Bert had put in me made me feel very humble and proud at the same time.

Bert said that the firm would find me a mate, but this rung alarm bells with me. Showing the best bit of common sense in my life I decided that they would most likely send me one of the elderly mates in the fleet, who would take no notice of my instructions and land me in trouble.

A pal of mine, Ray Green, who had been barging, was out of work in Colchester and so I sent him a telegram. "Join George Smeed as mate immediately," and three hours later he was aboard. Greenie was my own age and when I took him to the hospital to see Bert, Bert gave him a good talking-to. "Although you are both the same age, Jim is the skipper, and a barge can only have one skipper."

Ray took this all on board and never gave me any trouble, and we are still mates to this very day. We worked very well together and

Ray Green - my pal 'Greenie'.

started to earn ourselves some decent money. Greenie, feeling flush, decided to buy himself a new suit. When we got to Aldgate where the Jewish tailors worked, he bought himself a splendid wool suit for three pounds. In those days of course there were no synthetic materials. This sum cleaned us both out so the tailor kindly gave us the bus fare to get back to the barge.

The first opportunity for Greenie to wear his suit came when we were anchored off Heybridge, and he went ashore for a night out. He was convinced that with his smart new suit and white shirt with a high starched collar he would pick up the best-looking girl in Maldon. As he left in the dinghy to get ashore, I warned him to make sure that he got back before the tide fell too far. "Alright," he said, and off he went.

He must have had a very good night because he forgot the time, and when he returned to the dinghy it was no longer afloat but sitting on the mud. He had no option but to traipse through the mud in his best threads. I had turned in when I heard him climbing aboard by the leeboard, and the next morning I saw his suit laying in a muddy puddle on the deck. I roused him from his slumbers as there was a fresh northwest wind blowing and we were bound for London. Once we were underway with a good turn of knots down the river, I asked him how he was going to clean his suit? His solution was simple- "I think I'll tow it behind us for a while to wash some of the mud off."

He reeved a piece of rope up one trouser leg and then through the sleeve of the jacket and tied a bowline. The suit was towed behind us at six knots all the way to Gravesend. I grew concerned; "Isn't it time you pulled your suit in, Greenie? it has been in the water several hours, and the water is beginning to get dirty up here."

So we pulled it aboard, and when he held it up one leg was three feet longer than the other. In disgust he chucked the whole lot overboard, and thus ended Greenie's dreams of sartorial splendour.

Greenie eventually decided to apply for a skipper's job himself and he wrote to M. F. Horlock at Mistley, asking to be considered for a skipper's position. He was invited over for an interview, but was never very comfortable with face-to-face meetings. Although he would make a proficient skipper, facing the Guv'nor with three or four senior skippers unnerved him. His interview unfolded like this.

Greenie decided that he had messed up his interview so much that he might as well give silly answers and enjoy himself. One senior skipper barked at him, "Look 'ere, young man, suppose you're laying in Sheerness in a gale of wind and the anchor starts dragging, what do you do?" "Well, I'd chuck out another anchor sir." "Ah yes, but I am talking abaht a real winter gale, and your anchor keeps a-dragging." "Well, I'd chuck out another anchor sir." The senior skipper was not deterred and went into top gear. "You have got an oil refinery astern of you," he shouted, "If you bump into that you'd blow up half the Medway towns - what are you going to do now?" "I am going to chuck out another anchor sir." The owner intervened as the discussion degenerated into farce. "Where are you getting all these anchors from, young man?" "Same place that he is getting all his wind from, Guv'nor!" replied Greenie.

In spite of this interview Greenie did get a job, and they gave him a barge called the **Millie**. He did a good job, but had one failing- he would never ring up the guv'nor and tell him where the barge was. Consequently the office would enquire of the other skippers if they had seen the **Millie**. This lead to the barge being nicknamed H.M.S. **Millie**, or Horlock's Mystery Ship **Millie**.

Meanwhile, I had to find myself another mate to replace him on the **George Smeed**. I then signed on two mates who shared the job, on the understanding that the first one to get another job would leave. Having loaded a cargo of wheat for Felixstowe, we

George Smeed deep-loaded with wheat, bound towards Felixstowe. We always stowed our jib to the bowsprit; not rigged at this moment as we have a fair wind.

were running down the Swin in a gale of wind. It was very rough and in truth the **George Smeed** was a leaky old barge. Both mates ended up below being seasick, and I was left to sail the barge on my own. As well as steering, I kept having to reduce sail as the wind was increasing.

As we approached Felixstowe I decided I could get her through the pier heads, although with hindsight I should have anchored outside until the wind abated. I headed for the narrow entrance of the dock, still carrying perhaps too much sail and unaware that water had been taken aboard. As I approached the Pier Heads the huge amount of water in the bilges ran forward and the barge ran off the helm, ie. no steerage. As a result the barge hit the south pier head. Luckily, because the piles were so rotten they crumbled easily and made a nice soft cushion for the **George Smeed**. Several other barges were tied up there and their crews helped me manoeuvre the **George Smeed** around the wreckage of the pier and into a berth. At this point it was possible to see how low she was in the water with her deck for'ard awash.

I was concerned as to whether I had holed the barge by hitting the Pier Head or taken on sea water through our tough time in the Swin. With her under the elevator ready to unload we got the pumps working, and after an hour she appeared to be dry with no more water apparently coming in. However, I sat up all night to make sure that no leaks started again. I then realised that she was not holed on the pier head, but had been strained by stress of weather in the Swin.

The next day I caught a bus to Ipswich to visit a solicitor (Notary Public) to lodge a protest. This involved swearing an affidavit that being caught out in such rough weather the barge had leaked and may have damaged the cargo. The affidavit ensures that the skipper cannot be charged with damaging the cargo through negligence, and the insurance company will pay for the damage.

I returned to the barge for unloading, and the top of the cargo was still golden wheat. However, two feet from the bottom, the wheat had been soaked with seawater and was rock hard. We had to use pickaxes to break it up, and it had to be sent for pig meal as it was unfit for human consumption.

Hedley Farrington, and Jane Benham, aboard the **Memory** in 1963. Hedley was a true friend to the young skippers.

I then went to the firm's Colchester office, expecting the sack after demolishing the pier and ruining part of the cargo. Josh Francis, the owner, and Hedley Farrington, senior skipper, interviewed me. I explained what had happened with my heart in my boots, and expecting the worst. At the end Hedley Farrington looked across at Josh and said, "I think we put this down as a nursery problem, guv'nor." "Yes," said Josh to me, "You got yourself into a muddle but sorted it out yourself. By lodging that protest you ensured that the insurance would pay for the damage." Josh passed around the Players cigarettes and we all had a smoke to celebrate.

I staggered out of that room not dismissed as I had expected, but with compliments ringing in my ears. If only mishaps always turned out that way.

On another trip, whilst I was still only 18 and during my early days as a skipper, I was ordered up to the Surrey Commercial Docks to load timber for Creeksea. There were thirty-two standards of 'catch weights', which meant all sizes of timber and I would need a good stow to get this much timber on board. We always had to clear the whole consignment, even if it meant sailing with a huge and unstable stack above the deck.

This was in the 1950s, and the dockers were getting very militant. One little upset seemed to cause a strike, and a strike often meant that the whole Port of London would come to a standstill. It was like walking on broken glass.

I was loading out of a big ship named S.S. **Ljubljana**. She was moored off the quay on the Brunswick buoys, which meant that

craft could load from her from both sides. I was at her number four hold, and the sets of timber started to come over and into the barge. There were four dockers to a gang in the hold of the **George Smeed** and their job was to stow the timber in a safe and seaworthy manner. I became very alarmed when they began to draw the strops and simply leave each set in a heap where it stood. I remonstrated with them and threatened to call the

The tramp-steamer
S.S. **Ljubljana**.

Board of Trade in to oversee the stowage, a threat easily made and possible but with many implications.

One docker took exception to this and demanded money for a decent stow, and furthermore threatened to bury his timber hook into my face. Suddenly, with no further warning, he went into a red rage and rushed out of the barge's hold and charged towards me. I had nowhere to run and did what a frightened rat would do- I dived straight at him with my full body weight. When I hit him he was just about to step over the fore horse and was not very well balanced. He fell back into the rigging which caused him to turn and fall headfirst into the dock. Upon surfacing he clung onto the leeboard head fender, looking very frightened. I also was very frightened but determined not to let it show.

It was a very great relief to me when his mates pulled him aboard, but what was to be my plight? Would they all set about me, I wondered? Thankfully they didn't. He, now cold and dripping with water, had lost all his old bravado and like most bullies was revealed as a coward. I can picture him to this day climbing up the Jacobs ladder onto the ship with water still pouring from his clothes.

I still had a huge problem: no timber was coming over and I had three militant dockers on deck. I didn't think they would work with one member short in their gang. There seemed to be a long silence; then the ship worker looked over the ship's side and shouted, "Well, what are you going to do then?" After another long silence, one of the three replied, "Send one over." This meant that they were going to carry on working, albeit with no fuss about being one man short in their team. I was amazed and overjoyed and hoped that this might be the end to a very worrying incident. I immediately sent the mate below to make the three dockers a cup of tea and soon got chatting with them.

It seemed that their erstwhile colleague was not very popular and that he bullied and caused trouble where ever he went. They were as happy to get rid of him as I was, and told me that he had only just got out of prison for chucking his mother-in-law out of the bedroom window. They were sure that they had seen the last of him now.

My first command, the **George Smeed**, belonging to Francis & Gilders.

Typical of the Cockney humour, they knew that Colchester United Football Club had recently beaten Huddersfield and Bradford who were big at that time, so they kept shouting out, "Look aht, we've got a bit of a Giant Killer dahn 'ere." Needless to say I got a perfect stow, made friends with three rough but perfect gentlemen, and only I knew how nervous I had been throughout the whole affair.

I skippered the **George Smeed** all that winter of 1951-2 until Bert, having recovered from his broken arm by Easter, returned as skipper. Expecting to resume my duties as mate, I was surprised when Hedley, our ship's husband, there to help skippers and to make sure that they were provisioned aboard with everything they need for their vessels, revealed that **Mirosa** needed a skipper and offered me the position. I was reluctant to leave Bert as he was expecting me to be there when he got back, and I felt a great loyalty towards him. Hedley insisted that the time was right and with summer coming I should have my own barge. Two good friends, John Kemp and Gordon Hardy, agreed with him, and John, Gordon and I went to see Bert in Southend to break the news.

Mirosa whilst she was still called the **Ready**, prior to her name change.

I kept trying to bring the conversation around to barging matters, but dear old Bert was much more interested in showing me his onions and the rest of his garden. My mates were getting increasingly annoyed with me, but I could not bring myself to tell Bert about the **Mirosa**; I just funked it! John and Gordon glared at me and eventually we left for home.

As we were crossing the road, Bert called me back. "I heard that **Mirosa** needs a skipper and I recommended you." I was greatly relieved that he already knew and approved. I need not even have made the trip to Southend; dear old Bert.

Quite a lot has been made of the fact that us young men who rose to become skippers of sailing barges in the fifties came along at just the right time. The war had been responsible for creating an age gap in the normal order of advancement, and the younger skippers bridged that gap just in time.

In a stiff breeze, **Mirosa** makes a fuss through the water as she piles on the knots during the 1954 Medway Barge Sailing Match.

I heard two bystanders on the quay; one explaining to the other that these ships could be sailed by an old man and a boy. His companion was astounded to hear this, and the former confirmed with me, "That's right, isn't it, young man?" "Yes, that's quite right," I replied, whilst his partner queried, "So are you the boy, then?" "No, I'm the old man," I replied.

Although I was very proud of being promoted to skipper at such a young age, it brought me problems that I was too inexperienced to expect. The mates no longer regarded me as one of them, whilst the long-established skippers thought of me as an unproven whipper-snapper, and did not accept me as an equal either. They would glare at me, and one would say to the other, "Give 'im the winter – that'll sort 'im out!" Acceptance was a slow process as you had to prove yourself many times. Perhaps you would be lying in the Lower Hope with the weather a bit naughty and trying to decide whether to make a passage or not. Standing on the ladder to see what the other barges were doing, you did not want to get underway prematurely and make a fool of yourself. Any trouble

that you got yourself into would pass around the fleet very quickly, and be in the office in no time. Therefore us young skippers would always let the 'old uns' go first, then follow on after showing due respect to their experience.

It was a wonderful day when one of the old skippers, viewing the weather from his cabin hatch, would shout across, "What do you think on it?" This meant that you had been accepted because you were included in their considerations. You would give a cautious reply like, "Not a bad forecast, should be okay," because you did not want to appear cocky. He might then reply, "I think I will have a go." It was a warm feeling to know that you had been accepted into the brotherhood of Barge Skippers, a very exclusive club.

However, a word should be said of the younger mates who served us. They knew full well that they couldn't expect to be spending many years in

Mirosa leaving the River Colne in autumn 1953.

sail, yet these fifteen and sixteen year olds showed a responsibility, enthusiasm and competence that marked them as being out of the ordinary. Luckily, a boom in the coastal shipping trade came along which ensured for most of them a successful future; and no doubt their early days in sail were a great help to them.

Mirosa(R) and **George Smeed** pass Osea Island in a stiff breeze, having delivered timber to Sadds at Maldon.

Chapter V

The Sailing Barge Preservation Society

The Sailing Barge Preservation Society was born from an idea first conceived during the time I was skipper of the **George Smeed**, laying at anchor up the Shore Ends whilst on passage to London. It was the year 1951; on board was my mate Tommy Hawkins, and two friends, Colin Leggett, and John Kemp, who were making the passage to London with me.

After supper the conversation turned to a discussion on how much longer could the sailing barge survive in trade. The picture looked very dismal since grants and lottery money were unheard of in those days. The consensus was probably not long, since motor barges were already taking the cream of the work, and with their big open hatchways and more reliable delivery they were bound to win in the end.

We pondered about the possibility of the sailing barge being given a bit of extra help to extend their working life. Perhaps a few merchants, sympathetic to the sailing barge, could be persuaded to put some of their freights into at least one preserved sailing barge. This on its own would not be enough. However, if there was a society of members subscribing and providing for her long term upkeep the extra support would make her future viable. The talk went on into the early hours and by the time we got underway we only just saved the ebb down the Whitaker.

I was full of excitement of a sailing barge being saved as it had been jammed down my throat about sailing barges being doomed to near-extinction. I kept thinking about my old skipper's words, "Don't you moind they ole motors boiy they 'ont last, I'll tell ee fer whoy, thar all agin nature, thuss for whoy".

The seed was sown, but it was to be another four years before enough interest was aroused and the Sailing Barge Preservation Society was formally launched.

The barge chosen by the S.B.P.S. was the **Memory**, and it was only a coincidence that at this time I was skipper of her. I had been sailing the **Memory** for Horlocks and we felt that she was the right choice.

Horlocks very generously sold her to the Society for the sum of £1,125.00, and furthermore undertook to manage and operate her within their own fleet. This suited me very well; I really enjoyed working for Horlocks, and it meant little more than a change of flag.

The flag was a red background with a yellow never-setting sun. The citation read 'Bringing memories to the old and lessons to the young.'

The grand launching of the Society was organised by Eastwoods Ltd., the Brickmakers, and took place with the **Memory** moored off the Embankment. Close astern was moored the Honourable Company of Master Mariners' vessel **Wellington**.

The date was fixed for the 15th May 1956. Eastwoods, using their city connections, had somehow managed to get the Lord Mayor of London, Alderman Cuthbert Ackroyd, to perform the commissioning ceremony. We had to work to an exacting timetable as the Lord Mayor was lunching with the Queen at 12 midday, prompt - very prompt, we were made to understand.

Memory moored on the Victoria Embankment, dressed overall, in preparation for the launch of the Sailing Barge Preservation Society. With H.M.S. **Wellington** ahead, and Waterloo Bridge in the background.

The Police boat arrived carrying the Lord Mayor and his attendants, all in robes and tri-cornered hats. As we helped them on board, the embankment was lined with many onlookers as Eastwoods had publicised the event well. The **Memory** looked at her very best, having spent two weeks being painted and gilded at Eastwoods dock at Lower Halstow in Kent especially for this ceremony.

The Lord Mayor made his proclamation and then was ready to pull the cord to set the bob flying. Horror- where was the cord!? Where else but 8 feet up the ratlines, where John Kemp had tied it for safe keeping overnight. John then had to do an inelegant climb up the rigging to retrieve the cord in his posh city suit, all a bit bizarre.

The cord got duly pulled and the 'never-setting sun' waved in the breeze with much applause from the onlookers ashore.

The mate, Mick Alexander, and myself then conducted the Lord Mayor around the barge, first to the forecastle and then the hold. John Kemp joined us in the cabin where the four of us drank a toast to the Queen in traditional Pusser's Rum, sitting down of course which is absolutely right when on board ship. This tradition goes back to the Royal Navy, where in the time of sailing ships the King gave permission for the Royal toast to be drunk seated due to the low height of the deck beams causing numerous head injuries to his officers.

The Lord Mayor was over the moon at learning this bit of tradition and it was said that he used it as his party piece that very same afternoon.

Memory, behind me in the barge's boat, at Lower Halstow for a paint-up before going to London for the 'big day'.

It is worth mentioning that a barge's flag is normally sewn to a frame and flies free all the time. However, for this special and once only event, we thought it important to have the flag aloft but furled and then broken out when the cord was pulled. I got a Scout Master to show me how to do this, and learned the system thoroughly. Every time we set this up on deck it worked perfectly, but when we tried it aloft it failed. This was the day before the ceremony, and in desperation I climbed aloft and sat on the truck and furled the flag. I called down, "Right, now try it," and yes it was perfect. We had dozens of rehearsals and provided that I furled it from up aloft it never let us down. We had our last rehearsal at 11 p.m. that night and it was another perfect performance, and sitting 90 feet up on the topmast truck, I am sure I heard 'A nightingale sing in Berkeley Square'.

Memory in the 1930s, before purchase by Horlock, was always smartly turned out, as seen here when owned by the Ipswich firm of W. Christopherson.

Whilst we were at the Embankment, painted up and dressed overall, Everard's sailing barge **Sara**, similarly got up, was laying on the south side on the Festival of Britain site.

Unfortunately, when the chairman at Eastwoods, Mr. Miller, retired, so did that company's interest in the society and eventually, as you will read in the pages which follow, it was wound up. The money from her sale was donated to H.M.S. **Foudroyant**.

Much later, at John Kemp's funeral, with the Sailing Barge Preservation Society all but forgotten, I made the Society's flag to drape over John's coffin to commemorate all his previous hard work.

It is worth noting that us younger skippers, having been brought up in a rough environment, did not treat our mates to the same trials; I simply accepted the responsibility of going aloft on this exacting job as my own. Our young mates would still go aloft in the normal course of their work for the purpose of stowing the topsails or such like jobs.

Our generation of skippers, as young mates, all took pride in being totally competent, not yet thinking of ever being skippers. We taught ourselves a series of useful knots, we could splice wire or rope and were able to climb to any part of the rigging, setting up competitions between ourselves. Going aloft was also a recreation to be enjoyed and we would often be in the rigging for a couple of hours or more, just for the fun of it. One such challenge would be going hand over hand up one vang (on a barge pronounced 'wang') and down the other.

Some skippers would give a new hand a flag to put up as a form of test; if the bloke went home or refused, then he was considered no good anyway. This was my own indoctrination test, and though frightened at the time I felt my whole career was dependent on it. From that time on I could always get anywhere in the barge's rigging[7].

The best way to get to the flag was to set the topsail and to use the topsail hoops as a ladder. Going aloft in the bosun's chair was not the luxury that one might think, as when the chair had reached its top height and became chock-a-block you were still a long way below the flag, and worse still, in a sitting-down position. You then had to slither out of the chair, (which was just a small plank of wood which hung from four short lengths of rope coming to an apex), and stand on it in order to shin up the remainder of the pole to reach the acorn at the very top of the spindle. This had to be unscrewed to allow the flag frame to be removed. The old flag had to be cut off and the new one sewed on before refitting the acorn. Descending was an absolute nightmare, getting back into the chair was extremely hazardous; I go cold thinking about it now. Thank God for the modern harnesses; but bargemen never even thought of that.

Peter Horlock was one of the most able climbers that I knew; if he put a new flag up, he would first set the topsail and climb up the hoops as described earlier, but he would be one step ahead of the rest of us as he had the good sense to take his sewing gear and the new flag with him. He would then sit in the crutch formed by the headstick and the topmast and sew the new flag on, thus only going aloft once.

[7]: *This was a skill I kept up all through my sailmaking career, which was useful in taking accurate measurements.*

Chapter VI

Mirosa

To return to the narrative, once Bert had taken over the **George Smeed**, that left me free to take command of **Mirosa**; it was now Easter 1952. She had been launched in 1892 as the **Ready**. However, Trinity House wanted the name for one of their new tenders at Harwich and bought it. The guv'nor said to the then skipper, Billy 'Bundick' Austen, "We are going to lose the name **Ready**, so what shall we call her?" Billy replied, "Well, your daughter is called Rosa, so why don't you call her Mirosa?" Thus 1946 saw her name changed to **Mirosa**. The old men who had known the barge before the name changed would never call her by her new name, but referred to her as "'Er what used to be the **Ready**."

The Trinity House tender **Ready**, which took the **Mirosa**'s original name, served the Corporation from 1947 to 1977 and was the last steam 'yacht' in their service.

The chap who was charged with arranging the name change of the barge had been blinded in the North Atlantic convoys when his ship was sunk by a German U-boat. After the war, at a reunion, he met the German U-boat captain. The captain was so moved by the Englishman's plight, which he had indirectly caused, that he donated the cornea of one of his own eyes. They both spent the rest of their lives with one eye each. Although nations might have been at war, sailors the world over have a common bond which transcends nationalism.

My first cargo in **Mirosa** was English wheat, which was loaded at Fingringhoe Mill to be taken to the Co-op Mill in Victoria Dock. I had no mate, but John Kemp, my younger brother Brian, and Gordon Hardy, mate of the **Lady Helen**, were going to spend the Easter with me. I loaded up before Easter, and we sailed down from

Fingringhoe Mill and anchored off Brightlingsea for the night. Two other barges lay there with us. One was the **Repertor**, skippered by my old pal Minnie Maynard, and the other one, **Verona**, was skippered by Monty.

Mirosa, at Colchester, waiting to get away once Everard's collier, coming up astern' is moored up. She will lay just behind **Mirosa**, and the crane (belonging to the gas works) will unload her. Between the crane and the **Mirosa**'s mizzen mast can be seen my old friend Minnie's house. Note the barge's small yacht-like wheel, which she still has to this day, taken from the yacht **Artemis**.

We all went ashore to wet the new ship, as you would with a new baby. Traditionally I had to pay for all the beer that night, and we ended up plastered. This must have given me Dutch courage because it led me into making a stupid bet. As we came aboard the **Mirosa**, I pulled out five one pound notes and nailed them to the taffrail of the barge.

"The first one to beat me to Gravesend tomorrow can come aboard and take these notes," I boasted. This was a rash bet that I would never have made sober, because I was sailing a fully loaded barge and they were sailing empty. The starting time was supposed to be five o'clock in the morning. I laid on the locker all night, and woke at quarter past four and had a brew-up. I felt no compulsion to wake the crews of the other two barges who were still sleeping as we crept away at five on the dot on the last of the ebb. There was a fair easterly breeze once we had got through the Spitway. I then saw the tops'ls of two sailing barges just leaving Brightlingsea. They were punching the young flood which was going to take me up the Swin to the London river. Whilst they spent three or four hours tacking against the tide they stood no chance in hell of catching me, and of course I beat them to Gravesend and kept my five pounds.

It was the Easter Bank Holiday and so we had plenty of time to get up the Thames. On the Sunday we sailed up to the Royal Victoria Docks where John Kemp and Gordon Hardy had to leave me. John was going back to work at Bentalls, and Gordon was going back to join his own barge the **Lady Helen**. She was having an engine fitted at Rowhedge, and this left me to do a trip with just my young brother who was on holiday from school.

Before Gordon left he said, "I wouldn't mind coming mate with you, Jim." I replied, "Be careful Gordon, this barge only carries 100 tons and has no engine, whilst the **Lady Helen** now has an engine and carries 130 tons. You'll be able to earn much more with her." Gordon then said, "Well, like you I want to stay in sail." We agreed that he would go back to the **Lady Helen** and give in his notice, and join me when I got to Ipswich. When Gordon handed in his notice to his skipper Fred Pettit, Fred, who was a steady old boy, thought that he had lost his marbles.

When I arrived at Ipswich and unloaded, I paid off my young brother whose school holidays were at an end. This was the first money that he had ever earned.

Gordon then joined me as mate and thus began a long partnership which led to a lasting friendship. Gordon was a bit older than me, and the **Mirosa** was a fast barge, known as the slipperiest bit of wood afloat, and with such a very shallow draft it was reckoned that she would float in a heavy dew.

A voyage up to Marriage's East Mills, or 'poking up the Mill', was a more exacting job than just quanting along on the tide. You only had enough depth of water to reach the mill on a spring tide, and you needed to be of no more than six foot draught. On top of this, two of the four bridges between the Hythe and the Mill had very low headroom, so a minimum of air draught was equally important. Hence, this work fell to the smaller barges, who were commonly known as 'East Millers'. **Mirosa** was ideally suited to this work, and was of the 500 quarter size (112½ tons). To give ourselves the best chance of getting to our destination, we would load our cargo in London 'level keel', drawing, say, 5'11" both forward and aft.

Once we'd got to the Hythe we would lower the mast, and this would alter our trim a bit to perhaps 6'1" aft, and 5'10" forward.

Billy Austen at the wheel, Dick Banyard on the port bow, **Mirosa** 'poking up' to Marriage's East Mills, Colchester.

The trip up to the mill was a mile and a quarter, and the river bed, in that distance, would rise up three foot. We started from the Hythe the minute we came afloat, usually about 1 hour 20 minutes before high water.

Each skipper had his own mark, such as a nail in the wall, or a bolt hole in a pile. Some skippers, being a bit anxious, would run a wire out and literally heave the barge from her berth with the windlass. First you would pass under the Hythe road bridge, the lowest bridge of all, with the mast lowered completely flat so that the highest part of the barge was the top spoke of the wheel. We would have two hufflers on board, one on each side of the foredeck (some hufflers brought their own personal setting booms with them rather than use the barge's own motley gear). The mate would have another setting boom, and would work the main deck, port side, whilst the skipper steered. As you would be going up as fast as the tide, you would hear the rudder trailing on the gravel stones of the river bed.

The two railway bridges were of no consequence, as they were relatively high. The final one at East Mill was an arched bridge with very little water under it, and you might just slide through. By this time it would be about high water, and if the tide had not made its height, the barge may stop, grounded right in the middle of the bridge hole, and only yards from its unloading berth. If this happened, and the mill manager was on the ball, he could open the mill pond sluice, and the suddenness of this rush of water would raise the level by as much as two inches for just a few moments, thus giving us just time to reach the sucker. If this failed to work we would try again on the next tide.

It was on one such occasion, with the barge stuck right in the bridge hole and the ebb already away, we all agreed to meet again on the next tide which would be at 3 a.m. In order to go home for a few hours, we would put the barge's ladder up to the bridge parapet; we then climbed up the ladder and over the wrought iron railings on to the road. It was in the dark very early hours of the morning that my old skipper Arthur Rook, retired and in his eighties, and now my huffler, approached the bridge. Just as he was about to climb over the railings, a police car suddenly drew up. The policeman jumped out and said, "No you don't, old fella!" Arthur retorted, "Oh yes I do, I've got a barge down there!" The officer was most relieved to know that Arthur wasn't going to do away with himself.

Coming down empty presented a new set of problems. You now drew less water, but had more than increased your air draft. In the normal order of things, you would heave above the mill and swing in the mill pond, and then heave back to the bridge. You were still far too high to fit under the bridge at this time, and whilst waiting

Cargo discharged, **Mirosa,** her gear lowered again, waits to 'poke down'. Note how flat her gear has to be in order to get under the bridges.

for the tide to fall would be the time to get your mast down. Again, most skippers also had their own marks on the quay there to give them the right time to let go. This was all easily achieved, except in the case when you'd got as many as five barges at the mill, some loaded and unlikely to float. This would get all the skippers having a confab. Bold statements would be made- "It's no good you moving 'til I'm out your way," etcetera, and all the skippers agreed on a decisive plan of action. That was, until tide time, when all hell broke loose, each skipper running out wires and heaving his own barge about, with much swearing; but let's say you extracted yourself from the situation on this occasion.

With the tide having fallen the best part of three feet, you would let her go through East Street bridge and down the river; empty, you would only have one huffler. St Botolph's railway bridge was high enough to be of no consequence, but the next railway bridge now presented a bit of a problem. Remember, we had gone up to the mill loaded and as near level keel as possible but, when empty and with the gear lowered, the barge would draw about 3'2" aft, and only 1'10" forward, which meant that the ratio of air height to draft was greater than when loaded. This being so, we had to pause just prior to this bridge to allow the tide to go down a bit more.

The only possible way to stop was at a land drain outfall, which was surrounded by a small but strong timber pier. The mate would have to chuck a check line over one of the piles and, easing her stem up to the railway bridge, bring the barge slowly to a halt. When in light trim, the highest part of the barge would be the bitt heads. The measure this time was to let her go when you could put your fist, with thumb upstanding, on top of the bitt head and clearing the underside of the bridge. This allowed you to be at the Hythe bridge, the lowest bridge of all, where there was nowhere to catch a turn, still afloat and with clearance under it. Now almost on the ground, you would slide into the 'alley berth', and moor up ready to heave up the gear.

As mentioned, some barges were much easier than others; two in particular did have a serious mishap. The **Millie** had been built by Stone's at Brightlingsea and was never intended for the East Mill work; nevertheless, the skipper, 'Nosmo' King, thought she would get up there and therefore fixed her for a freight on one occasion. She had in her time had high bitt heads put in, with the traditional thumb cleats on top. He was advised to saw these off before going up the mill, which he did, and made one hell of a mess using his blunt saw. She got up to the mill all right, but coming down was the problem; trying to get under the Hythe bridge, the stern actually got aground, and the barge stopped right in the middle of the bridge hole. They thought they could solve the problem by turning the fore hatches upside down, battening in the tarpaulin and filling the hollow with water. They then pulled the boat up on the barge's bow and filled this with water. As the next flood tide came, they were ready with the winch handles to heave the barge through, and it looked as if they were going to be successful when, all of a sudden, the boat on the bow capsized and spilled all the water out.

The barge now raised herself up enough to jam under the bridge, and unfortunately this was of course the flood tide. The fire brigade had to be called immediately to fill her with water, and thus save both barge and bridge from serious damage. She was eventually extricated, but never attempted to return to East Mills. Her sister ship, the **British Empire**, being owned by Francis & Gilders, was in fact a regular trader to East Mills; Tom Simmons, her skipper, was very experienced in the East Mill work and could manage well enough. Nevertheless, years later, when she had an engine fitted, her trim was altered and she came to grief just as the **Millie** did.

We continued the East Mills work, carrying wheat from London to Colchester, and various cargoes to Felixstowe and Kent; in fact to anywhere that was needed. All was going well with Gordon and I, and we shared many laughs together. The summer of 1952 was particularly pleasant although with long calm days and little wind. As a consequence we would often be drifting along the Swin when we would encounter a lovely excursion 'steamer' called the **Royal Sovereign**, with its complement of boisterous cockneys on an outing to Clacton. They would hang over the

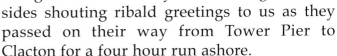

sides shouting ribald greetings to us as they passed on their way from Tower Pier to Clacton for a four hour run ashore.

By the time they passed us again on the return journey with their 'kiss me quick' hats we had only drifted six or seven miles in the light wind. Gordon suggested that perhaps they thought we were pirates and we should give them a show. "What if we chase each other round the deck with choppers?" he pondered. "Not likely," I replied; if anything happened to one of us on the way up to London there would be sixteen hundred witnesses on the **Sovereign** who had seen us chasing each other with choppers!

The excursion 'steamer' **Royal Sovereign**.

However, we did have fun teasing the Royal Navy on occasion. As we were sailing past Southend one day, we saw an aircraft carrier anchored off the pier. Although we did not normally carry an ensign in the mizzen peak, we hoisted a dishcloth or anything else we could lay our hands on so that we could salute the Navy by dipping our 'flag' as we passed. We would wait until we were right alongside them before dipping.   This would catch the officer on watch by surprise as he would not be expecting a salute from a humble barge. He could not allow the Navy to be outdone in the politeness stakes, so he would order an unfortunate matelot to dip their ensign in return. The sight of some poor seaman sprinting the length of the flight deck to perform this duty before we passed them would fill us with delight.

As well as having some harmless fun like this we took a great pride in our barge, sometimes using our own money buying paint and varnish to keep her in a condition that we would be proud of. One day we were sailing along the Maplins, and Gordon was scraping the wheel prior to re-varnishing it. I went down below to have my lunch leaving Gordon steering the barge. An hour later I emerged after a rest on the locker to find that both the wheel and Gordon were missing. Aghast, and wondering what was happening, I looked for'ard to see Gordon scraping the wheel on the forehatch. I called to him, "What are you doing up there?" "Well, I came up here because it was sunny," he replied. The barge was still sailing along in a straight line without a wheel, a remarkable tribute to her sterling qualities.

On another occasion we thought we would clean up our brass bell and unfortunately it was not made of brass but gunmetal. Gunmetal has a dull look, but I purchased some chemicals from the chemist who assured me that they would bring up the bell nice and shiny. We put the bell into a brand new galvanised bucket and poured on the correct mixture from the chemist. The whole thing bubbled and hissed so alarmingly that I was concerned it might overflow and burn through the hatch cover. Gingerly, I put a boat hook through the handle of the bucket and transferred it carefully to the stone quay. The next morning the bell looked as dull as it always had, but our shiny new bucket had had all its galvanising removed. This rather damped our enthusiasm for renovations of this type, and in future we decided to stick to paint jobs, which were only undertaken between freights.

Marriage's Felixstowe mill, known as the East Anglia Flour Mills. Motor Barge **Viking** is under the elevator with sailing barge **Spinaway C** alongside.

Six months after my eventful trip into Felixstowe as skipper of the **George Smeed**, when the barge hit the pier head and demolished it, I again found myself approaching Felixstowe in a westerly gale. However this time it was not a southerly gale in a leaking barge with both crew below seasick, but in a well-found barge with Gordon, my very competent mate. Felixstowe dock was just a basin and the barge had to be stopped dead once inside. We approached fast even under bare poles, and once in the piers I went hard over with the helm and Gordon touched the anchor on the bottom. I got Gordon to back the fores'l with the bowline on, and we drudged in alongside the mill without cracking the proverbial egg.

That night Gordon went ashore to have a drink at the local pub, and got chatting to the mate of a Lowestoft trawler that was moored in the dock as well. "Are you the mate of that barge?" he asked. "We saw you come in this afternoon in the gale of wind; lovely job of handling her I must say. What age is your ol' skipper?" "Well, it is his birthday tomorrow," replied Gordon with a grin, "he will be nineteen." I felt that my previous disastrous arrival with the **George Smeed** was now expunged by our performance with **Mirosa** that day.

On another occasion, we were bringing wheat to Cranfields at Ipswich and again it was blowing quite hard. The tide had not made enough for us to lock in at the Pier Head and so we had to moor up to the large buoy outside and wait.

Mirosa, a slippery
bit of wood!

This was quite a tricky operation, and involved running one of our best mooring ropes from the stern along the deck and up to the bows. As the bows came alongside the buoy, which was shaped like a huge barrel, the mate had to jump onto it and make the rope fast. The rope would then be used to check the barge and slow it to a stop before it hit the Pier Head. It is not possible to stop a seventy ton barge laden with a hundred tons of wheat quickly without parting the rope and doing some serious damage.

We were travelling rather fast past the buoy when Gordon jumped onto it, and by the time he had made a bowline the barge had passed and he had no time to jump back onto the stern. There was nothing I could do at this point, as I was busy checking the barge with the pier head looming up before us. As the rope became taut the buoy was dragged through the water, spinning as it went, and covered in weed and slime. Gordon did a terrific job of barrel-running on top of it to keep up, just like a circus performer, and I was very impressed. I was even more impressed when the mooring chain of the buoy became taut, and the buoy stopped abruptly - but Gordon didn't! He executed a neat double salco, a triple lutz, and followed with a deft Indian death spiral into the water.

By the time I had made the barge fast Gordon had swum back and climbed aboard without any difficulty, because we were deep-laden. "Sorry, Gordon," I said, "I was going to fetch you in the boat." "No problem," he spluttered, "My dad taught me to swim when I was very young. Getting out of the sack was the hard bit!"

Our work on the **Mirosa** did not really earn us enough money because she was a small barge and could not compete with larger barges carrying more cargo. To make matters worse, when we were laying in London and our turn for a cargo came, if it was too large we would have to give up our turn for a bigger

Mirosa, at Woolwich in 1948 with a stack of timber.

barge. We would be left languishing on Woolwich buoys with no work or pay, as we were only paid by the cargo that we carried.

This was a depressing time and would eventually lead to a lethargic attitude, and we would spend as much time as possible painting the barge. Some skippers, during a sojourn on the buoys, would send their mates aloft in the bosun's chair and have them scrape the topmast. This was really just to keep the mind occupied, which was an alternative to playing cards in the foc'sle, which, given the chance, the mates would probably have preferred.

To eke out our work, we would often load ballast from Fingringhoe to London even though it was poorly paid. On one occasion we went to the Freshwater Sand and Ballast Company to load a freight of ballast. A barge called the **Vera** followed us in, skippered by a chap nicknamed Bugle 'cause of the size of his nose. As I had arrived first it was my turn to load, but there was insufficient water for me to go alongside the jetty. Bugle came on board and asked me if he could take the first turn, to which I replied, "No, as my turn is my living." As the tide flowed I got my anchor and set my sails to sail into the berth and was surprised to see Bugle start his engine and try to rush me. Fortunately the **Mirosa** was a lighter draught than the Vera and I slipped safely into the berth whilst **Vera** hit the mud and lost the opportunity to pinch my turn.

Once loaded, I sailed down to Brightlingsea where the wind was blowing a full gale. I anchored and lowered the topmast, and got the second anchor ready to let go. The **Vera**, which had loaded after us, went by at about 10.30 p.m. under engine. I thought this was not very advisable with the strength of wind blowing, and we put our second anchor out before turning in for the night.

The next morning we found our mainsail had been damaged, although tightly stowed up, by the strength of the wind even though we were lying at anchor. Switching on the radio at 8 a.m., we heard that a Thames barge had been lost in the Thames Estuary. We had no doubts that it must have been the **Vera** (see page 32), and we were right.

The **Vera** had sunk just inside the Maplin Spit. Bugle had got her into as shallow water as he could, and he and the mate climbed the mast as she sank. With all other lifeboats out that night, only the Margate lifeboat was available to help them. The coxswain had to land the lifeboat on the hatches of the sunken **Vera** in order to rescue her crew. He used a large wave to get off again, and took the survivors off into Brightlingsea as it was the quickest way of getting them help. They were pretty well done in after a night in the rigging, and could not have lasted much longer. The lifeboat coxswain received a Silver Medal and a Vellum Citation for his work that night, and well deserved they were. When I met Bugle twenty or thirty years later he was still raising money for the R.N.L.I.

'Starvation Buoys' at North Woolwich, 'urchins' on the foreshore.

There was often no work, barges laying idle on Woolwich Buoys, better known as 'Starvation Buoys', waiting for the freight market to pick up. The foreshore urchins (of whom Nobby Malthouse was one), who never seemed to come to any harm, would always say, "Can we look after your boat mister?" You might just as well say yes, as they'd take it anyway the minute your back was turned. They were simply local kids, and this was their natural playground. They probably got a good hiding each time they got home as they were usually covered in mud.

It was apparent to Gordon and I that our time with **Mirosa** was coming to an end. We just could not earn enough money with her, although we both loved sailing her from London to our home ports in Essex and Suffolk.

I wrote to the firm of M.F. Horlock & Co. of Mistley, who had a very good fleet of sailing barges, to see if they could offer me a position as skipper. By the time I got to Maldon, I found there were three letters waiting for me, which I opened in the date order they were posted.

MANAGERS FOR F. W. HORLOCK'S OCEAN TRANSPORT CO., LTD.

M.F. Horlock & Co Ltd.

SUCCESSORS TO FREDK. W. HORLOCK

SHIPOWNERS · BROKERS · FREIGHT CONTRACTORS

TELEPHONES:
MANNINGTREE 26
ROYAL LONDON 2633
IPSWICH 3558
TELEGRAMS:
FRED. HORLOCK, MANNINGTREE.
CEKARRIER, BILGATE, LONDON.
COASTWISE, IPSWICH.

MISTLEY,
MANNINGTREE
ESSEX
CODES: SCOTT'S 10TH EDITION · BOE

ALSO AT
4, NEW LONDON STREET, E.C.3.
KEY STREET, IPSWICH.
DIRECTORS:
M. F. HORLOCK (MANAGING)
C. C. DALTON . . . . . .
B. HORLOCK . . . .
S. M. HORLOCK . . . . .

OUR REF.   YOUR REF.   DATE

JHA/BEG.   October 28th. 1953.

Mr. J. W. Lawrence.,
22, St. Lenards Road,
COLCHESTER,
Essex.

Dear Sir.,

        In reply to your letter of the 26th inst, we can

definitely offer you either the "REPERTOR" or "PORTLIGHT" and

shall be pleased to know when you can enter our Employ. We

presume you can get Mate.

        Yours faithfully,

One of the three letters offering me various barges. The paper is quite thin, and the letterhead is beautifully embossed.

One offered me either of the steel barges **Xylonite** or **Repertor**, the second one offering me just the **Xylonite**. I was not interested in either of these barges, as they were both known to be very unhandy when loaded. However, the third letter offered me the steel barge **Portlight**, a barge I knew to be handy under all trims, light or loaded. Like the others, she was relatively modern, built in 1926.

I was still in a quandary about leaving the **Mirosa** when I telephoned Horlocks. The phone was answered by a man I did not know who had a somewhat abrupt telephone manner. "Hello, this is Jim Lawrence, skipper of the **Mirosa**, calling about **Portlight**." "Well, do you want her?" "Well, yes." I replied, rather taken aback by his directness, and still not sure that I wanted to leave **Mirosa**. "Well get over to Ipswich and take her over." cried my new boss, and promptly put the phone down.

I went back on board in a rather subdued state, still unhappy about leaving the **Mirosa** and a way of life that I had come to love. Gordon was much more positive about the **Portlight**. "Jim, you know what it is like when we are stuck in London with no work. There is plenty of work with Horlocks. What are we waiting for?" When I phoned up Hedley Farrington at Francis & Gilders, my employers, he said "You go, Jim, this is a great opportunity for you."

Hedley had been a very good friend to me. I said that I would give him a freight's notice. He said, "No Jim, there is not much work about. When you are unloaded sail the **Mirosa** back to Colchester and leave her there, and that will leave you clear to join the **Portlight**."

So with very mixed feelings Gordon and I cleared and scrubbed every inch of the **Mirosa** - grub cupboards, Yarmouth Roads and both bunks, cleaned out the foc'sle and swept the hold clean. This was the traditional way to leave a barge ready for a new crew to join.

The sail down the Blackwater from Maldon to Brightlingsea was very nostalgic and a little sad as I knew that we would not be working these rivers very often in our new ship. We then sailed and towed up to Colchester and said our last goodbyes to the ol' girl there.

Mirosa on Francis & Gilders' barge yard, just above Colchester's Hythe Bridge. We have set the barge away from the quay in order to scrub and tar round.

Opposite: **Mirosa**, out of trade and beautifully preserved, seen here competing in the 1985 Blackwater Sailing Barge Match.

Chapter VII

Portlight

Horlock's **Portlight**, captured in a tattered amateur photograph from the period, setting a little mizzen staysail, when her hull was black, a livery she had but briefly.

We arrived in Ipswich Dock the next day and found the **Portlight** amongst a dozen other barges. She was of course locked up, so we dumped our gear on the deck. I then went around to the office of the Ipswich Steam Ship Company, who held the keys to the barge. They were a subsidiary of Horlocks, although there were no steam ships owned by them at this time. The office was run by a very efficient lady named Margaret, who soon found the keys. Margaret could have been aged anywhere between 18 and 35 years old, and all the bargemen fell in love with her, but she had the good sense not to sleep with any of them!

In Ipswich Dock with **Spinaway C** inside her, **Portlight**'s rust-spattered hull in need of a good lick of paint.

Horlocks had told her that I was coming, and Mr. Allison, the Company Secretary at Mistley, was very concerned that there was no coal on board. We never bought coal because the Thames was full of coal which we traditionally 'borrowed' for our own use. It was very necessary because a steel barge is much colder than a wooden one. I told Margaret that I would like 1 cwt. of coal delivered to the **Portlight**. By the time I got back to the barge, 5 cwt was being delivered. I thought, This is going to take the shine off our first freight before we start. However, once we got to Mistley, the guv'nor had paid for the coal at no cost to us.

There we were on our first morning on **Portlight** with coal and our bedding scattered around the deck, when we received a visitor. It was George Feint, skipper of a motor barge **Orinoco**. He said,

"Congratulations on your new command. Do you want a pull out of the Dock?" "Look at the mess I am still in." I said, but he was insistent. "I'll come alongside and give you a pull down to Shotley."

We duly arrived at Shotley and anchored for the night. Shotley was a good place to start from the next day. With us were the **Memory** and the **Anglia**, apparently both windbound. The next day it was blowing hard from the southwest. George Feint was taking his barge the **Orinoco** out and suggested that I go and give it a try. I agreed and we were soon underway.

Portlight empty, half mainsail set, heels easily to the stiff breeze.

The **Portlight** was so different from the **Mirosa** which had much more beam and was very stiff, and all of her gear would creak and groan. The **Portlight** had a beam of only 18ft and would lean over much more in the wind. However she would go through the water like a witch and there was no weight on her gear. The spray was coming over the bows giving us an exhilarating sail, leaning so much you only needed a stump for one leg.

I gave the wheel to Gordon whilst I went forward to check the gear, my first opportunity since taking over the **Portlight**. It was all strong and sound, and I had no misgivings left. Neither did Gordon at the wheel with a grin on his face which went from ear to ear! We both realised that we had a very good barge, very different to the **Mirosa** but each craft unique in her own way.

We both liked the **Portlight** very much, and we were kept busy sailing from London to all the ports up the Essex and Suffolk coast for the next three months. When we eventually got to Mistley I walked into the office; Mr. Allison, who I had only spoken to on the phone said, "Can I help you?" "Yes, I am the skipper of the **Portlight**." "Ahhhh, at last we meet," he cried, and he turned out to be a most charming gentleman. I got on with him very well and we became friends.

We continued working hard and made a lot more money than before. Gordon would open his wallet and without counting the notes would exclaim, "I am down to my last quarter of an inch in pound notes - time to get in another freight."

Portlight laden, water on her lee deck, Gordon Hardy at the wheel, shore transport laid on the main hatch.

Our partnership lasted until I received a telephone call at Leigh-on-Sea from Hedley at Francis & Gilders. He asked if I thought Gordon was ready to become a skipper. Although I did not want to see him go I reluctantly replied that he was ready. Apparently Bert was retiring from the **George Smeed** and they needed a new replacement.

Squared off before the wind, **Portlight** sets nothing ahead of the mast, nor her mizzen, but makes good speed through the water.

When I told Gordon about the call and got him to ring Hedley, his feet did not touch the ground. He returned from his telephone call jubilant and excited, and said, "I've got it! When can I leave?" "Well you can leave now if you want, I should be able to pick up another mate here." So off went Gordon that night to join the **George Smeed**, but of course we always remained very good friends. I remembered the **George Smeed** from my days on her as a leaky old barge, and Gordon joked, "I will have to sleep with one leg dangling out of the bunk, so that when it gets wet I know that it'll be time to start pumping." I managed to get a new mate and was able to continue working as before, although I did miss Gordon.

I have mentioned anchoring and getting underway many times, which. of course, involves heaving the anchor up. For those who are unfamiliar with the mechanics of a barge's windlass, a few words of explanation. The barrel of the windlass is made of wood, albeit with a strong iron bar through it, and is about four feet across. It is octagonal in section, and spiked onto the barrel are planks of wood known as whelps. They are in fact sacrificial pieces, and can be renewed from time to time when worn. In order to work correctly each plank needs to be made of alternate types of wood, one of elm then one of softwood, eight in all. This allows for the correct amount of grip for the anchor chain, together with the ability to let the chain slip, but only under your control.

The anchor chain is rove twice round the barrel, though it looks like three turns when viewed from above, and is then led out through a snatch at the stem and shackled onto the anchor. The two turns around the barrel provide quite sufficient friction to stop the anchor from running out. The bulk of the chain, usually about 30 fathoms, is carefully ranged abaft the windlass, with another 15 fathoms stowed below; 45 fathoms in all[8].

8: *Around 83 metres, around 3x the barge's length.*

When preparing to anchor, sail is reduced and the mate wets the windlass barrel. This actually reduces the grip. When the skipper shouts "Let go," the mate throws an additional bucket of water over the barrel then physically throws chain over the windlass, perhaps as much as three or four fathoms, and then gives the next turn a start, and down goes the anchor. He continuously keeps chucking chain over and in only a few minutes the barge is laying to anchor on fifteen fathoms.

A sailing barge's anchor windlass, with bucket handy.

To heave the anchor up, the windlass is geared, and two handles can be fitted. As you heave up, the turns of the chain work their way across the barrel; you then have to stop winding in order to 'fleet' the chain over to prevent riding turns. Fleeting is done by pulling back the chain that has just been hove in and throwing turn number one as far as possible across the barrel. With a deft flick, which takes a bit of practice, you can make the other turn jump across. More chain is then hove in until it is time to fleet again. It usually takes three fleets to heave in fifteen fathoms, and this gives a little respite from heaving. Once the anchor is off the ground, fleeting the chain safely can only be done using the dog to grip the anchor chain.

The 'dog', a forked claw secured to the deck by a light chain, is engaged on an anchor chain link from underneath, taking the load once the chain is slacked for fleeting across the windlass barrel. The moment the load on the anchor chain is re-applied, the dog drops to the deck ready to use again.

Our lives were ruled by the direction of the wind. On one occasion we had unloaded at Mistley, and I was ordered to London light. I had a rotten 'fluey cold at the time and as I went home on the bus to my mother's house, where I still resided, I thought I would give myself a couple of days in bed to recover.

The next morning my mother brought me a cup of tea in bed and said, "Jim, the wind is straight up the garden." I was out of the bed like 'a rocket out of a silo' because this meant an easterly wind; a breeze fair for London. Rushing back to Mistley I had reached Wrabness before I had my next cup of tea, my 'flu forgotten. If the wind had been south-westerly I would have languished in bed for a couple more days.

When I returned to my mother's house two months later, she asked if I had recovered from my cold okay. "What cold?" I replied. To a sailorman, a fair wind is the best cure for the common cold.

Chapter VIII

Sweet Memory

Seen here when trading, **Xylonite** did herself proud in the 1953 Match, a very different and more glamerous role when compared to her regular work.

It was not all work and no play. In the early spring of 1953 there was talk of reviving the Barge Match, which had been suspended since the duration of the war. As this was also the year of Queen Elizabeth's Coronation, the race was titled The Grand Coronation Barge Match. At this time I was still trading in the **Mirosa** with Francis & Gilders, who didn't enter, but Horlocks did, and entered the **Xylonite** in the Champion Bowsprit Class. She beat the **Sirdar** and came home in second place to **Sara**, not a bad performance for a trading barge against two barges preserved for racing.

By 1954 I was in the **Portlight**; it was decided that Horlocks would enter **Memory** for both the Thames and Medway races in the Champion Bowsprit Class. There was also talk of the skipper of the **Memory**, Lionel Horlock, retiring, and Jack Allison said to me, "Jim, I think you should have the **Memory**."

The **Memory** was a fine wooden barge, but I was reluctant to leave **Portlight** as I had got her to a standard that I was proud of. She had a good suit of sails and sound leeboards. Also, we had an open order to go and load ballast at the Freshwater Sand and Ballast Company when our own work was slack, and although ballast work was poorly paid, it at least gave us a freight up to London, which helped keep the grub locker full. Ballast work was okay for a steel barge with no keelson, but would not have done for a fine wooden barge like the **Memory**.

Tilbury Dock plays host to (L-R) Horlock's **Xylonite**, their ex. sailorman **Resourceful**, the **Memory** and Everard's **Sara** with her very last cargo.

"Thanks; I think I will stay where I am." I replied. But Jack pressed me. "No, you will do better in the **Memory**, Jim, give it a try. You will lose nothing." I was still not convinced because by now I was used to the sailing properties of the steel barge, although I loved wooden barges.

Jack then told me that **Memory** would be entered into the Thames and Medway races. "Dick Creswell and Pincher Bloyce are to be co-skippers, with Monty, Peter Horlock and you as crew. There will be five of you racing and when the race is over you are to be her regular skipper." "What about her sails, Jack," I inquired, "they ain't up to much." "Don't you worry about that, she's going to have a new suit of sails for the race, and fully refitted, so she'll be brand new when you start with her, Jim." "Okay," says I, at last persuaded as my final objections were overcome.

The name **Memory** was given to the barge after the man who originally ordered her, Bob Haste, unfortunately died before she was completed.

The race was a big commitment for a small company with just ten barges. With five skippers crewing the **Memory** this left half the fleet laying idle. When we got to Gravesend we could see that events had moved on. Our two main rivals, the **Sirdar** and the **Sara**, the reigning champions, had now been fitted out with huge racing gear. The **Memory**, although very well found, was still a trading barge. It would appear to be a 'millionaire's game' between The London & Rochester Trading Company and F.T. Everard & Sons.

Everard's **Sara** to leeward, the London & Rochester's **Sirdar** to windward, as their crews push these race-rigged flyers in the battle for victory.

Sara took the cup beating **Sirdar** by twenty-one minutes, but **Sirdar** beat **Memory** by only three minutes. **Nelson**, the fourth barge in our class, was left out of sight. Two days later the Medway race provided a similar result.

Horlock's never raced in the Champion Bowsprit Class again, sensibly leaving that to the millionaires. After the two races we sailed **Memory** back to Pin Mill, where the race crew left to return to their own barges. I was then joined by John Impey who was going to be my regular mate.

Opposite: **Memory** in splendid form, racing under the Horlock bob, hot on the heels of the specialist racers.

After a short spell at Ipswich to repair some race damage we returned to normal trade. John was not yet sixteen but was a splendid mate with a cheeky sense of humour. I was stowing the foresail on one occasion, though in the old days this would have been strictly the

mate's job. I could see young 'Imp' was out for a game, so before turning over the last fold I chucked him in and put the gasket round. I pulled the foresail half-way up the stay and there he was, cocooned, with only his head sticking out. He was still laughing. Nevertheless, we took the job seriously enough and kept the barge well maintained in between voyages.

Sara invariably beat **Sirdar** and remained the overall champion. In 1955, Sirdar came out with huge new gear and new-style Dutch leeboards. **Sirdar** beat **Sara** in the Thames, and thrashed her in the Medway race. Was **Sara**'s reign over? Alf Naylor was Everard's sailmaker, and he was on the **Royal Sovereign** Committee Boat with his boss Fred Everard. He said, "It will take a **Veronica** to beat that **Sirdar** now, guv'nor". The **Veronica** was once reckoned to be 'the fastest bit of wood afloat.' However, seven years before, she had been badly holed in a collision and left to rot, full of mud and with grass growing out of her; a sad fate for such a splendid barge.

Looking very unlike one of the most successful racing barge of all time, **Veronica**, seen hard at work, discharging her cargo at some remote sea wall.

Fred Everard did no more than rush to the bridge of the Committee Boat **Royal Sovereign** and demand a radio telephone link call through to his yard. The terse message was, "Dig the Veronica out." His men were in the mess hut drinking tea when the message came through, and their reaction was "DO WHAT?!" Before the end of that 1955 race, men were in the hold of the **Veronica** digging the mud out of her!

In 1956 **Veronica** entered the race resplendent in white enamel paint and much gold leaf. She now had a huge hollow 66ft sprit, with a bowsprit 45 feet long, more than half the length of the barge, and Dutch-style leeboards. **Sara** was likewise equipped.

Veronica proved her worth over the next eight years, invariably outsailing Sirdar, breakages and mishaps excepted. **Sara** never seemed to find her old speed again, although all three barges were very fast. By 1963, even the big companies racing their barges were feeling the pinch and announced that this was to be the last commercial barge race. The London and Rochester Trading Company always had Kentish crews in the **Sirdar**; Tommy Cooke, Jimmy Diddams and such. That year, in a hell-bent effort to win the two races they relented and chose one of their other skippers, an Essex man named Jack Pettit.

Jack's dad had been the first skipper of the **Sirdar** when she was new in 1898. Jack had originally been third hand on the **Sirdar**, then mate and eventually skipper, and he had great faith in her. Currently Jack was skipper of a motor barge, the **Marie May**, and he began to choose his crew for the race. I regarded it as a great compliment when he asked me to sail with him on **Sirdar**. After all, I was an Essex man working for a Suffolk company, and I was surprised when The London and Rochester Trading Co. agreed to me joining the crew.

We met on board two weeks before the race to practice. The 1963 Thames race was the fastest ever sailed. **Sirdar**'s top speed was recorded at thirteen and a quarter knots through the water, but still the **Veronica** beat us, though we held off **Sara**. **Veronica** did the entire race at a smidgeon under eleven knots.

The Medway race gave a similar result. Two grand days sailing; we had done our best, but Jack still thought that **Sirdar** could out-sail the **Veronica**. However the curtain on the contest had now come down for good.

A staggering transformation, clouds of cotton canvas extend from **Veronica**'s spars to catch every breath, as she races downwind.

I asked Chubb Horlock, **Veronica**'s co-skipper if, given a few more years, Jack could have improved the **Sirdar** to a point that she could beat **Veronica**. Chubb replied, "No, Jim, because every time Jack could find a little extra speed in **Sirdar** we could find a little extra speed in **Veronica**." That was Chubb's honest opinion, but he had his crew together for eight years, whilst Jack only had his crew together for one.

Dreadnought racing, when I.C.I. owned, with her trading rig.

Jack was 60 years old when he raced **Sirdar**, and I did not see him again until his ninetieth birthday. As soon as I walked in, he left the group he was talking to at the other side of the hall and strode over to me, saying excitedly, "You know what we done wrong don't you?" He then reiterated the whole race and pointed out a different strategy. When he had finished I said to him, "Well we won't make that mistake again next time, will we Jack!" He died three months later.

On race days the owner would provide the crews with large quantities of provisions because we could not cook whilst racing. There were large joints of ham and cooked meats, huge cheeses and large fruit cakes. With the abundance of food there was inevitably large amounts left at the conclusion of the race.

Dreadnought, then Everard owned, in her 1958 racing rig - note the size of her gear and staysail.

One skipper thought this a terrible waste, and put some of the food in his kit bag ready to take home after the prize-giving. Unfortunately, he was observed by some apprentice boys who, once he had departed, removed the food and replaced it with lumps of wood. When he returned later he took his kit bag home, where he discovered the joke that had been played on him!

Memory did not race again until 1958, when she flew the flag of the Sailing Barge Preservation Society who had bought her from Horlock's. However, she was still under management to them, therefore the only change for me was the flag.

We could not afford the fitting-out costs for the Champion Bowsprit Class and so entered for the more modest Restricted Staysail Class. **Memory** stood a very good chance in this class; her closest rival was the **Dreadnought**, and both barges were closely matched, two fast but near-equal contestants. We then heard that

Dreadnought had been bought by Everard's, who were up to their old tricks. They had fitted her out with a huge suit of sails from **Sara**'s spare gear, with Bob Roberts as their skipper. This was a formidable combination and we certainly had our work cut out. On the plus side, I had the famous Nobby Finch on board of pre-war racing days, also Mick Lungley, together with my current regular mate, Micky Alexander. I was confident enough that we could give a good account of ourselves.

When we got to Gravesend, the **Dreadnought** was a sight to behold with a huge staysail, big enough to take your heart away. 'Let's hope it blows hard enough for them to be unable to set it.' was our sentiment, but it was not to be. The Thames Match was held in fine weather and the **Dreadnought** beat us, but only by one barge length.

The Medway race was a different kettle of fish, with a fresh wind all day and continuous rain. We tacked our way down the Medway with the wind in the north-east. Once outside the Garrison, I could see that the **Memory** would be better off without her staysail. I was also watching the **Dreadnought** and could see that her huge staysail was knocking her head off the wind something alarming, more of a hindrance than our own much smaller staysail; they were also sheeting the sail into cleats in the waist and could not harden them in. By contrast our own staysail sheets were lead back to the crab winches, which gave us full control.

I.C.I. also entered **Revival** in the Thames and Medway races, and this picture is a particular favourite of mine. She is being sailed here by 'Trunky' Shepherd. With that clean wake, I would recommend him as one of the finest barge helmsmen.

Memory competes
in the 50th Medway
Barge Sailing Match
on 12th June 1958.

Nobby shouted from aft, "Jim, drop that stays'l, it's doing more harm than good!" "Yes, I know it is," I replied, "but not as much harm as **Dreadnought**'s staysail is doing to her. You know that Bob will never ruck first." Therefore we both hung on, although both barges would have benefited by the absence of their stays'ls, with **Memory** surely going ahead. Once around the

West Oaze buoy we ran for home. **Memory** could run like a witch, and despite her standard size staysail against **Dreadnought**'s huge one, they could never catch us and Nobby steered us home 14 minutes ahead.

As well as the winner's cup we also took the cup for seamanship. I met Bob in the gents toilets after the prize-giving and Bob said, "Well fair do's, Jim, one each." He held out his hand which I warmly shook. As we both stumbled out of the door I said in my drunken stupor, "Bob, shouldn't we have washed our hands or something?"

It is so sad to think that **Memory**, one of the finest examples of a Cann-built barge, should finish her days prematurely, compared to some of those still surviving today. Especially so when one considers the dedication of the men who built her and the quality of their workmanship, proven by the many thousands of tons of cargo she carried safely in her life.

Hulked in Tollesbury saltings, **Memory** was abandoned there in the 1990s.

Chapter IX

Red Sail Network

Although these days marine transceivers are commonplace and allow easy communications between vessels at sea, this was not the case in the 1950s. Our only communication was bellowing across a strip of water between our barges and boats, or hand signals.

In 1957 a group of us barge skippers solved this problem in our usual unconventional and slightly illegal way. We travelled to Lisle Street, Soho, where it was reckoned you could pick up anything, and bought some army surplus shortwave transceivers. We installed these in seven of the remaining sailing barge fleet. We had the help of a T.V. boffin at Ipswich, when T.V. was still in its infancy. He described our radios as being oversized hearing aids. He produced an aerial using coaxial cable, but we rarely got more than a two mile range.

Unlicensed transmitters were strictly forbidden and so we had to decide on code names for our call signs so that we could remain anonymous. At this time the soap powder giants were waging war on one another on Radio Luxemburg. Advertisements from the likes of Alan Freeman, such as "Hold it up to the light, not a stain and shining white." were constantly ringing in our ears. That's it, we thought - let's call ourselves after the soap powders.

I chose to be Omo. Gordon Hardy became Tide, and others would be Daz, Dreft, Lux - we even had a 'Brand X'. So in the twilight years of the sailing barges at least some of the barges had radio contact with each other. This was nicknamed the Red Sail Network.

On one occasion my B.B.C. wireless receiver broke down when it was nearly time for The Archers. What a panic there was - I frantically got on the radio. "Omo calling Tide, come in Tide." Gordon Hardy replied "Tide." He suggested, "Jim, put your earphones in your pudding basin and I will put my microphone close up to my receiver and relay the programme to you." Ah, the

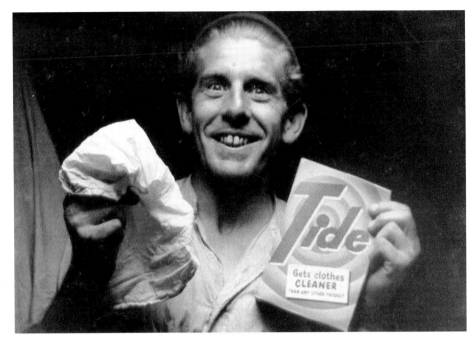

Gordon Hardy, skipper of the **Portlight** by this time, chose Tide as his radio call sign.

wonders of technology. My mate and I leaned over the pudding basin and enjoyed the whole of the fifteen minute episode. Old Walter Gabriel was as good as ever.

We had no idea what channels or wavelengths we were transmitting on. Mick Lungley reckoned that he had listened to a T.V. cricket commentary whilst somebody else thought they had tuned in to the Police Band.

Les Sadler had some small talk with what he thought was an aeroplane. When he heard the next day that a plane had been wrongly diverted from Heathrow to Gatwick he got the wind up and promptly chucked his set overboard. Where the rest eventually went I have no idea.

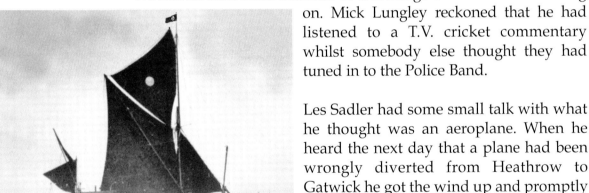

Spinaway C has brailed her mizzen, the signal to listen. Sometimes a pre-arranged time was agreed for listening to our 'traffic' on the airwaves.

I have often thought of some poor squaddie with one of these strapped to his back; they weighed about forty pounds and provided very poor performance. This is illustrated by the old story about the officer relaying a message back to headquarters through several of these short range sets. By the time it reached H.Q., his message, "Send reinforcements, I am going to advance," was transformed to "Send three and fourpence I am going to a dance."

Chapter X

Racing for Turn

Racing for turn was essential in the days of trading barges if the crews were to earn a living, since the first barge in would pick up the next available freight. When sailing by the share, laying idle, waiting for a freight, or sailing light meant no pay.

Before the days of engines, when all barges were under sail, it was the accepted practice to 'race for turn'. It was not entirely cut-throat as there were some unofficial rules of conduct. Barges racing up to London would take their turn in the order that they arrived at Gravesend, and barges racing down to Mistley would take theirs from the order they arrived at Wrabness. Likewise barges bound to Ipswich would take their turn from Pin Mill. This was on the owners' orders to avoid serious damage which would have been more likely when racing in the upper, narrow, reaches.

These rules had to be modified a tad as more and more barges had motors fitted but it still needed to be competitive. The rules then meant that if you started off first, whether sail or motor, and provided you arrived at your destination in time to take your turn, then your turn was guaranteed. If, of course, a freight turned up before you arrived then naturally it would not be held, but would be taken by a vessel already there, and you would go next in turn.

It was possible to lose your turn if a freight turned up which was too big for your barge to carry. Then a larger vessel, which was next in line, would be given the freight and the smaller barge would have to wait for a suitably sized one. But, if a big barge was next in line and a small freight was offered, then the big barge could retain his turn and take the small cargo. The reasoning was that a small profit was better than no profit and 'a bird in the hand is worth two in the bush'.

When a barge spent some time on the shipyard for repairs, the crews would only be on a small retainer wage. To compensate them, they could sail their barge to London and claim first turn before all others of that company.

Sometimes a skipper would use these rules to his own advantage. Dick Cresswell once pulled a fast one when five of Horlock's barges left Mistley ahead of him. He promptly went on the yard for a tide with nothing much wrong, then sped off to London to catch the others. He claimed first turn over the others, as he had "... just come off the yard."

Dick took his duties as a skipper very seriously and was reckoned to be a superb bargeman, but had the reputation of being a hothead. His **Reminder** was unquestionably the smartest 'ironpot' afloat. He once challenged the governor to find a pound of rust in total anywhere on the whole barge. I bet he was correct as well, as Dick would even chip the rust from under the rail capping, which was completely out of sight, because 'it was the right thing to do'.

Dick's sense of rightness eventually led to his undoing. One day in London he was completely at loggerheads with Jimmy Heywood, our London man. The dispute arose because he considered that our firm's motor barge **Spithead** had pinched his turn and it was not right. Without telling anyone he motored all the way back to Mistley to have it out with the guv'nor.

Unfortunately, shortly after his hurried departure a freight turned

The **Spithead** started life as the X-Lighter X44, a landing craft built in Sunderland in 1915 for the unsuccessful Dardanelles campaign in World War I. Despite her 100+ years, **Spithead** is still afloat as a houseboat in Kent.

up and no-one knew where Dick and the **Reminder** were. The freight had to be given away to Sully's to save it from being landed, which could have proved to be very expensive.

Another survivor, the other player in the dispute, Dick Cresswell's charge, Horlock's **Reminder** is, like the **Spithead**, still afloat, though unlike **Spithead**, is still active, now in the hospitality and charter 'trades'.

By the time Dick reached Mistley, he had cooled down, but the guv'nor hadn't. He was forced to leave, and by agreement of the other barge owners Dick was never allowed to take a barge in trade again. He had to go labouring on the rebuilding of the Cattewade Bridge to earn a living, a terrible waste of an excellent skipper.

Some years later he did return to the sea to take the Harwich-built **Gladys** doing corporate work. Without doubt Dick was one of the smartest of bargemen that I ever knew.

As the years passed, more sailing barges were laid up and now there were only seven left trading. Francis & Gilders had unrigged their last four barges including **George Smeed**, and Gordon Hardy had re-joined Horlock's as skipper of the **Portlight**. He had with him as mate young Frank 'Nobby'

Malthouse. Nobby, as a kid lived in Bargehouse Road, Woolwich, and was a regular London foreshore urchin. He made a splendid barge mate, a chip off the old block in fact. When our barges were alongside somewhere, some skippers and mates liked to have a means of transport handy. Quite often a bike was carried, or a Vespa motor scooter, even a Bond three wheeler once rumoured aboard Everard's **Cambria**.

Some barge skippers carried a motorbike on board and this was the case with Joe Trotman. He moored his barge up at Isleworth one Friday, and found the mill didn't want to unload him 'til the Monday. This gave him a good opportunity for a weekend at home. He swung the bike ashore, got into his leathers, and was ready to leave when Gordon Scott also stepped ashore with a view to catching the train. Joe said, "Come on Gordon, save the train fare – jump on the pillion with me."

It wasn't always possible for Gordon Hardy to get humans as mates - or is that Nobby Malthouse wearing a mask? Note the crew transport - a scooter on the cabin top.

Gordon had got no protective clothing and was dressed in his normal 'walking-out' overcoat. Driving through London, there was a sharp easterly breeze. Gordon started to cough, and tapped Joe on the shoulder saying, "It's no good, Joe, the wind's going right through me - drop me off and I'll go and catch the train." But Joe was having none of that. He stopped the bike at a bus stop and said, "Right Gordon, get that overcoat off." Joe then held the coat up in front of Gordon, saying, "'Ere y'are, put your arms in here." Joe then buttoned the coat up behind Gordon and put the belt on and turned the collar up over Gordon's mouth. "Right," said Joe, "Let's have another go." As they sped through the East End of London, Joe shouted over his shoulder, "Are you alright, Gordon?" "Yes Joe, I'm as warm as toast - turn the wick up!" he replied.

It was customary for Ipswich people to divert from the A12 at Colchester and go via Ardleigh, Lawford, Manningtree and Brantham etc. It made the journey two miles shorter. As they went round the bend at the Brantham 'Bull', the back wheel went from under them, the front wheel hit the grass verge and left the pair of them lying in the grass, not seriously hurt but very stunned. The customers at the 'Bull', hearing the commotion, ran outside to see if they could help. One old lady went up to Gordon and screamed "Oh look, this poor man's head is turned right round!" Had she looked closer, she would have noticed his feet had as well.

Us latter-day skippers might race against each other for pleasure, but we would always 'report in' our colleagues coming behind and insist that they got their rightful turn. You did not need to watch your backs in these latter days and we were a loyal and gentlemanly fraternity.

However, I remember once when I had to revert back to old-fashioned guile. I was skipper of **Marjorie** in charter work, bound for Maldon with only about one hour to high water. It

The magnificent **Marjorie**, built at Ipswich by millers R. & W. Paul in 1902, a credit to her present owner's determination to keep her in peak condition, her hull with a shine the envy of many a yacht.

fell a flat calm as one of the L.R.T.C. tin motor barges came up the river. I waved him a rope and he kindly came and got me in tow astern. He was deep-loaded and drawing about 7ft. By the time we got to Hillypool Point I realised that if he kept towing me he was not going to save his water up to Green's mill. We hailed him to let go the tow, but not once did he look back. I mustered all the charter group for'ard shouting to him, but alas to no avail. He still did not hear us. In desperation we bought all the empty beer cans from the galley dustbin and threw them onto his steel deck, but still could not attract his attention. The charterers enthusiastically drank more beer to provide more ammunition, but there was still no response.

The tide was now away and only when we were up to the Town Quay did he send his mate out of the wheelhouse to tend our rope. The mate must have been bewildered by all the beer cans on the deck as we neatly glided into our berth. The motor barge only managed another four hundred yards up the river when he ground to a halt on the bottom.

I sculled up to him in our boat and apologised; if he had not stopped to give us a tow he would have certainly made his berth. He was quite alright about it but said that he had particularly wanted to get home that night. In an agony of guilt, I offered, with the help of his mate, to take the barge up to her unloading berth on the night tide. He gladly accepted my offer and departed for home.

I then realised that I had talked myself into a predicament as I was sailing with another charter party on the next day tide. Since I carried no mate in those days, I used the charter passengers to help me sail the barge. However, there was only myself as dogsbody to prepare the barge during the twenty-four hours in port; I had to dispatch the leaving party, clean the barge, get in stores such as gas and paraffin for the lamps and all the sundries to keep the barge operating.

That night, early on the tide, I went up to the motor barge just before she floated. I prepared to start the engine, which was a Kelvin. This had to be started on petrol by injecting petrol into each cylinder head then physically turning it with a starting handle. Petrol continued to be fed into an air breather until the engine was running fast enough to switch over to diesel. This was normally a straightforward procedure, except when the air breather refused to take in the petrol because it was blocked. This problem was simple to resolve since there was a recess in the air breather, with a nipple which had to be removed and cleaned with a fine wire pricker. Due to problems of access a special tool was required to unscrew the nipple, and this was normally kept close to the engine where it could always be found. I asked the mate where this special tool was, but he replied that he did not know as the skipper always looked after the engine. It took so long to search for it, in vain, that when we went on deck again the tide had fallen and we were once more aground.

In despair I turned in on **Marjorie** for what was left of the night, and next day decided to abandon the motor barge's engine. I would order the tug to tow her to the unloading berth, then the tug would take me back to Marjorie and tow me away on the same tide. So the day tide found me on the deck of the motor barge waiting for the tug.

Suddenly I saw a sailing barge coming up river under topsail and half mainsail; she was loaded, and it was the **Cambria**, skippered by Bob Roberts. A cold sweat came over me - he was drawing a foot less water than the motor barge, which was not yet afloat, and our tug had not arrived yet. Bob would love to beat a motor barge to the berth, it would be worth another chapter in a book to Bob, but I was desperate to preserve the turn of the motor barge at the unloading quay.

On impulse, as Bob sailed by I called out to him in a friendly manner, "You can't go into the berth Bob, there are some rocks fallen over the side, I have left Hasler's berth clear for you." "Thanks Jim," he called as his mate got the rest of the mainsail up. The tug was soon with us, and I urged Dickie to quickly get us alongside of Green's and then get me away in the **Marjorie** as soon as possible. The charterers were amazed at the speed of our departure, with the shore lines chucked off and away we went. I showed them how to set the sails as we went along. Dickie towed us to windward, and then we let go of the tug. Paying away on the port tack, we then rounded onto the starboard tack to clear Herring Point and bore away down Basin Reach with the wind abeam.

The sailing barge **Cambria** seen here when in trade, the last pure sailing vessel to carry cargo in northern europe, now recently rebuilt and preserved in commission by a trust set up to ensure her survival.

I then sat on the cabin top steering and laughed my head off, swearing that it would be a long time before I took another tow from a motor barge. I did feel sorry for Bob though, and a couple of years later when he owned the **Cambria** I assuaged my guilt by making him a present of a good second-hand topsail and foresail; I am sure that I more than squared our accounts.

Chapter XI

Paid by the Share

Being paid by the share meant that we had no guaranteed wages, and did not get paid for sailing empty, or any holiday pay. There were no specified hours; Saturdays, Sundays and Bank Holidays were all in. However, you would handsomely share the freight money with the owner, and a very energetic crew could do well for themselves.

Typical employment conditions would be that the owner was to provide the barge, well-found, with sails, paint, cordage, paraffin oil for the navigation lights and to keep the vessel insured. The crew were to provide all their own personal gear, bedding, heating and food.

Good, but not easy, money could be made in the sailing barges. A deep-laden barge in heavy weather would always have water on deck, quite often swept from bow to stern by the angry North Sea.

When a cargo had been unloaded, the freight money would then be split in the following manner: Firstly, all the running expenses would be subtracted from the gross income, including brokerage, dock dues, towage and any miscellaneous expenses that had accrued to the barge in any way. The owner would then take 50% of what was left and the skipper would take the other half as the crew's share, of which he paid the mate one third. For example, if the gross amount was £70 and the expenses were £10, then the owner would have £30, the skipper £20 and the mate £10.

Taking the expenses out first meant that each party paid their own part of the running costs, which in turn encouraged the crew to go easy on the towage, and sail or heave with the dolly line wherever possible. There was one more payment, 'The Captain's Guinea', paid by the merchant to the master in order to encourage him to take special care of the cargo.

The crew might sail the barge to London, where most of the freights were to be had, or might be lucky enough to pick up a cargo from where they last unloaded. The merchants would be allowed five working days in which to load and unload the barge in accordance with the terms of the Charter Party. This was to limit the time taken and so avoid the crews spending long, unprofitable, stays in port. Once booked on, you started logging your days; for example, if it took four days to load, then there would be only one day left to unload the barge. If the combined loading and unloading took more than five days, then the merchant would have to pay demurrage in compensation for the delay.

Once on demurrage, the payments carried on over weekends and bank holidays. The bargeman's dream would be to lay loaded on demurrage over the entire Christmas period. The delivery rate remained the same whether the barge made a quick passage or lost time laying windbound. Surely what could be a better incentive to get on with it.

One day we loaded with barley in Felixstowe Dock, bound for Mistley. The hatch boards were raised above the coaming in order to increase cargo volume. Sacks were draped inside the hatches to avoid spillage and our 'stack' was well rounded on top to shed water once the hatchcloths were on and secured with rope breachings. As we were only sailing from Felixstowe to Mistley, we crammed as much cargo in as we could, and it was only a bit of bravado on our part, as each trip we tried to carry a bit more than the last. This involved loading until she got water on deck.

The most I ever got loaded into the **Memory** was 167 tons. Turning up to Mistley that day I was just off the Ballast Hill and as I was making a tack, we were struck by a terrific thunderstorm. The wind flew out from the north-west and with the barge stationary in the water, she laid over till water was almost running down the cabin hatch.

Memory just loaded with barley from storage sheds at Felixstowe, her iron band awash, bound to maltsters Free, Rodwell & Co. at Mistley, Suffolk.

As with most thunderstorms, there was one terrific blast and then a short lull before a harder blow came. It was during this lull that the **Memory** picked up a little speed and thereby regained her stability, but it taught me a serious lesson and I never loaded the covering board under after that.

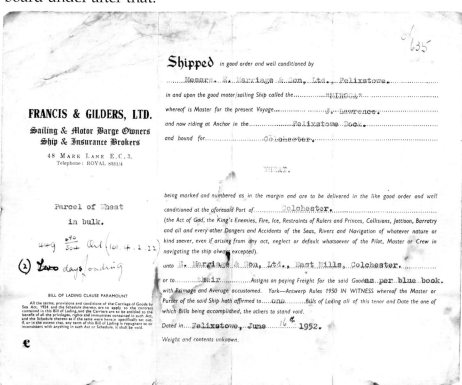

My Bill of Lading for bulk wheat from 16th June 1952 aboard **Mirosa**, consigned from Marriage's Felixstowe mill to their East Mills, Colchester.

Chapter XII

Farewell Old Shipmate

My old school chum and mentor, Minnie, had gotten himself married to a really lovely girl named Pat. On one occasion, he came ashore with her at Brightlingsea, and when they landed on the causeway it was a bit muddy. Minnie was wearing his long boots, whilst Pat was in a light summer dress and white slingback shoes. With no more ado, Minnie gallantly swept her up in his arms, just as a rowing boat landed at the causeway with three elderly gentlemen. They had been fishing, and each had a motley string of undersize mud flounders. Minnie presented Pat to their gaze and with a wink exclaimed, "You should have seen the one that got away!"

My very great friend Minnie.

Minnie moved away from sail and went into the motorised sand barges. They were in fact from a fleet of First World War landing craft and some were well past their best. The crews were encouraged to load them too deep without sufficient reserve buoyancy. This resulted in many fatalities, and it was only after a vigorous protest by a well-known sailor and journalist, Hervey Benham and, incidentally, my mother-in-law Mrs. Rouse, that a Plimsoll line (maximum load line) was introduced to these craft. Not without reason did the headlines read 'The rebuilding of war-torn London was mixed with the blood of Essex sailors'.

Minnie was skipper of such a vessel named the **Alpheous**. Minnie and Pat were proud parents of a baby boy named Stephen. Unfortunately Stephen was born with a hole in his heart, and had to be taken up to a London hospital. Pat, being a country girl, was not familiar with London and Minnie desperately wanted to go with her. He carefully worked out his freight schedule and decided that he would be home in time to accompany his family to the hospital in London. On 26th October

1956, Minnie and his mate, Jimmy Jewel, endeavouring to hold to their schedule, set sail into the teeth of a north-east gale from Brightlingsea, the **Alpheous** laden with around 192 tons of sharp sand; alas, they were never seen again. Minnie, with such talent, was only twenty-four years old, and Jimmy, a loyal and faithful mate, was around the same age.

At that time I was unloading wheat at Felixstowe, and can remember the ferocity of that northeast gale. By the time I had unloaded, the gale had subsided, but I could not depart as my regular mate was off sick.

However, I soon had a replacement in the form of young Barry Pearce, with orders to sail to London light. The wind was north-west, not a good wind to get out of Felixstowe Dock. Just as I was pondering a plan for departure, a launch from the Trinity House Vessel **Patricia** motored into the dock. She was carrying all the brass-bound officers, but the launch man I recognised as a young former barge mate. I waited until the big brass had gone ashore and then I waved a rope up to him. He quickly understood that I wanted a tow out of the dock and he would earn himself an extra quid into the bargain.

As he came over to take my rope I realised that he would be inexperienced at towing, so I called to George Cooper to jump into the launch with him. George was skipper of a little motor ship called **The Miller**. I said to George, "Make sure he holds me up to windward and not let me soak onto the lee pier head, and I will set the topsail as soon as it will draw." George had been in sailing barges most of his life, and with his experience and a bit of help from our topsail, the launch, with only a 14 horse-power

George Cooper's
The Miller.

engine, slowly towed us clear of Felixstowe piers. After letting go of the launch Barry and I sailed the **Memory** over to the Guard and anchored for the night.

We mustered at 5 a.m. the next morning and took the ebb tide out of the harbour. The wind was north-west Force 3-4 and the water was smooth, as you would expect with the wind in that quarter. The **Memory** was in her element as we took the flood tide up the Wallet and then bore away for the Spitway. I ran her off to clear the South Whitaker, when I noticed a strange disturbance on the surface of the water. "That's new to me," I said to Barry, "it seems most peculiar, so get the lead line out."

We sailed around that strange disturbance, but could not understand what it was, or what was causing it. We left it, feeling puzzled, and set our course up the Swin. We anchored in the lower part of the Thames that night and went up to the Woolwich buoys on the next day tide. Only the **Redoubtable** was moored there, and as we slipped alongside her skipper Tom Lancaster took our ropes. Once we had moored Tom exclaimed, "Minnie is missing." "Ol' Minnie will be alright, Tom," I replied. "He has broken down in some lonely old anchorage; he'll turn up."

I had such faith in the capabilities of my best pal that I could not ever imagine him lost, but the days went by and he did not return. On 2nd November bits of wreckage, 43 hatch boards, etc., were found on the north-east side of the Isle of Grain and the clincher was when two lifebelts with the name **Alpheous** on them were washed ashore there. Stunned and numb, I now had to accept the worst news I could have received. It was then that the strange phenomenon I had witnessed off the Whitaker came to mind, and I reported the facts to the P.L.A. and the Customs. They searched the area but found nothing.

Many of us were very disappointed; we felt that greater effort should have been made, and that there was enough experience and knowledge to have found any vessel in a known area of the Thames Estuary.

Well, you can make what you want of it but Barry and I were the only people to have witnessed that strange behaviour on the water. It has never been seen since, but somehow, whenever I make a passage up or down the Swin, my course always seems to lead me to that spot. I often wondered if my old mate was saying goodbye to me.

Chapter XIII

Enough to Make a Saint Swear

As I've grown older, I have realised that Josh Francis, my old guv'nor, together with all the other barge owners, had to cope with all the many and varied characters of the skippers in their barges. Some would be 'blow-hards', some steady but reliable, others always in trouble and breaking gear, but I think what made the thing gel together was the competitiveness between them. They were proud men, and no-one liked to be beaten by another skipper. By the very nature of things, we were all bested at different times.

The **Ethel Ada** and the **Lady Helen** were once laying at anchor in the Colne, empty, and both bound for London. They had two very hard skippers, who never let a chance go by.

One, Michael Bligh, was as hard as nails and sometimes considered impetuous. Although given a certain amount of respect, he was often referred to as 'Mad Michael'.

The other, Joe Mumford, could also push a barge hard but, always with great reliability. Joe's religious beliefs led to him being known as 'Holy Joe' behind his back. Joe was never known to swear, but would have his own temper words such as, "Oh, Marmalade and Mustard" and many more.

On this occasion, with the wind howling from the south-west, Joe knew that there was no chance of him making the passage. Michael, on the other hand, thought the wind showed a bit of west in it, and started heaving up. Joe's mate, standing in the companionway of the **Lady Helen**, reported this to Joe. Joe, unshaken in his prognostications, said, "Where the Jam and Marmalade do that mad fool think he is going? He'll blow the gear out of her."

However, Michael departed, and strangely enough, once he got outside of the Colne he did find the conditions better, and the wind had more west in it. He was able to carry his topsail, and made the Thames that night.

Joe, with the wind still howling, was convinced that Michael might have got up the Shore Ends, inside the Crouch, or at worst had broken some gear and had to run further to leeward to Harwich.

Michael, in the meantime, was in London and found a freight of wheat was waiting to be loaded for Colchester. With no let-up in the weather Michael had got it made. He had now got a fair wind for Colchester and it could blow as hard as it liked.

Francis & Gilders' **Lady Helen** safe and secure alongside at Colchester, her skipper no doubt champing at the bit to be after his next freight.

As Michael and the **Ethel Ada** approached the Colne, Joe's mate, standing on the companionway ladder, relayed to Joe that a loaded barge was coming in. "I can't make out who it is yet." A little later he called out, "It don't 'alf look like the **Ethel Ada**, Joe." An agitated Joe exclaimed, "No, no, no, he ain't Mustard well got to London yet, let alone loaded." A little later still the mate was then sure, and called out, "Yes it's the **Ethel Ada**, I can read her name now."

At this Joe broke down and could take no more. "Oh Jam, Mustard, Marmalade, Fiddlesticks and *@?!# the **Ethel Ada**!" However, Joe still went on deck to give Michael a congratulatory wave as the **Ethel Ada** stormed past on her way to Colchester.

Chapter XIV

A Rare Case of Anthrax

I was laying in the Royal Albert Dock, waiting to load soya bean meal for R. & W. Paul of Ipswich, when notices appeared pasted up around the dock, telling you to beware of anthrax. They were luridly coloured posters, showing pictures of what the disease looked like on the skin. It didn't tell you what to do if you contracted it, as there was no cure for it anyway; just avoid getting it, advised the poster. It advised that it first showed up as a skin infection and the inference was that it was nearly always fatal. Close by was a ship in from the Far East.

At 8 a.m. the next morning, the **Mousme** went alongside and started to take in a cargo of 'hoofs and horns'. It was the most vile cargo imaginable, the left-over animal bones from butchers shops, restaurants, and abattoirs, with a fair bit of very putrid meat left attached to them. She was to load the cargo and take it to Sheppey Glue works to be boiled down for making into glue; the smell was not only in the nose but stuck like a taste in the throat. The stench would spread throughout the barge, through the bulkheads into the accommodation aft and foc'sle forrard. As soon as 'hoofs and horns' were brought into the dock, more anthrax warning notices went up with more strong colour pictures showing why contracting the disease was to be avoided.

She finished loading about tea time. The skipper said he was going home to Rochester for the night and would be back on board first thing in the morning to undock. The skipper was on board bright and early next morning, when the mate said, "'Ere, skip, look at my hand." The top of the mate's hand was covered in small blisters. The skipper recoiled in horror, the graphic pictures on the posters ashore very much on his mind. "'Ere," he said, "I'm getting you down to the seaman's 'ospital at Gravesend and let them have a look at that 'and of yorn." This suited the mate as his girlfriend lived at Gravesend and he thought he might get a chance to spend some time with her.

So they undocked and made their best time to Gravesend, where they anchored and the skipper put the mate ashore. When he returned from his supposed visit to the hospital the mate said "They don't know what it is, skip, I've got to see them tomorrow." The skipper said, "Right, I'm not staying aboard here with your 'and, I'm going 'ome and I'll see you tomorrow."

When he called out to the mate later the next day, the mate said, "They still don't know what it is, skip; I've got to go back tomorrow and have some more tests done." Once again, the skipper went home to Rochester. He was getting worried, partly because of what the mate's illness might be and partly because he hadn't yet told the owner of the barge's delay. The following morning he arrived back at Gravesend pier and hailed his barge; the mate called back. "It's worse today, skip, all the blisters have broken and me hand is all wet, and I've got to go to the hospital again this afternoon."

Just then a tug rounded up and moored on the pier; the mate of the tug leaned out from the wing of the bridge and called, "Hello skip, how's your mate's hand?" "We don't know" said the skipper, "and even the hospital don't know what it is." The tug's mate looked a bit surprised and said "Well I know what it is; when you was up the dock the other night he spilled a kettle of boiling water over his hand, that's what. Ha ha, I reckon he's having you on, skip; his judy lives ashore here."

The penny dropped as the barge skipper realised how he had been taken in, and said, "Oh, the little rascal him." (or barge skipper's words to that effect) and sacked his mate on the spot.

Another sacking with a happier outcome occurred when a barge was unloading at Cranfield's Mill in Ipswich dock one Friday. The skipper and the mate had been at loggerheads all day and by the afternoon it had developed into a row. This resulted in the skipper giving the mate the sack.

After they finished unloading, they pulled away from the unloading berth into a spare berth and they covered the hold. The skipper then went down to the cabin to get his kit bag in order to go home for the weekend. The mate went down the foc'sle, presumably to pack his gear.

Mirosa starts unloading at the Cranfield Bros. Ltd. roller mill at the top of Ipswich Wet Dock.

When the skipper came back on the Monday morning he found his barge wasn't where he left it. He eventually found it down on the pier head ready to lock out, all scrubbed round, ropes all coiled down, the tug alongside and his old mate sitting on the bow rail having a fag and talking to the tug skipper. "Oi!" said the skipper, "I thought I gave you the sack." "So you did," said the mate, "but if you don't know when you've got a good mate, at least I know when I've got a good skipper!"

Chapter XV

Nearly Quarantined

In later years the **Hydrogen**, having just completed a public relations reception for Bells Whisky at Southampton, the skipper decided to swing the barge in readiness to go to sea. It was blowing hard, and all he had to do was get a stern rope out and let the wind take her round. Just as her bow came alongside the quay, nobody noticed the one inch bolt sticking out, which pierced the barge just above the waterline. Shortly after this the agent arrived and told Steve, the skipper, that he was required back in London. Steve said that he had a problem with the barge as he had just knocked a hole in her, "but I can repair it myself, at least to get us back to the shipyard at Maldon. This is a list of the shopping that I need…" and the agent set off to go and find him one sheet of barge felt and one sheet of lead, both about 12" square, plus a 1lb. of felt nails and a gallon of tar.

Off went the agent on this errand, and returned about one hour later with everything except the barge felt. Steve said, "Well, mate, it is only to thicken the tar up, they used to use horse muck in the old days. Here, take this bucket and find me some horse muck."

As the agent was about to leave the dock, the exit was blocked by a large crane lifting a huge crate out of a ship. Inside the crate was a very agitated giraffe. He obviously did not enjoy being raised over the sheds and you can imagine the state the floor of the crate was in as it landed. The agent said to himself, 'Well I do not really know where to get some horse muck from, and I am sure that what is in the bottom of that crate will do just as well'. Once the crate had landed he nipped over with his bucket, filled it to about three quarters full, which he then put in the boot of his car, and drove back to the **Hydrogen**.

As he pulled up alongside the barge, so did two other cars. One was the Customs Officers and the other was Immigration

The big mulie **Hydrogen** in the Thames when undertaking the Bell's Whisky promotional charter.

officials. They immediately confiscated the bucket and its contents, and enquired as to what the agent intended doing with it. He said that it was to repair their barge with. "Luckily, you didn't," said the Custom's man, "That giraffe and the contents of that crate are all going into quarantine for six months. Had you have used it on your barge she too would have had to be quarantined for the same period."

Chapter XVI

Weather Warnings

It always intrigued me as to how the old skippers could foretell the approach of bad weather and I was determined to learn all I could from them on this subject. There were many omens, the moon on its back, or a big star near the moon. Even a nice day was looked upon as a weather breeder.

One old boy used to go on deck to relieve himself and would come back down the cabin and say, "Ah, there is some bad weather about, I can feel it in me water." Everything was a bad sign, and a gale was always imminent, but still they went, saying, "If we get out of this without a pasting, we'll be very lucky." Eventually a gale would come, and they would nod knowingly and exclaim, "There, I told you so!" so they were in fact always right.

That's not a bad philosophy, it meant that you were always alert and looking for something that you did not want to see. Slowly I came to realise that a red sky at night only meant that the shepherd's hut might be on fire.

There is no doubt that a good barometer was your best bet; if carefully watched you could find a twelve hour window and therefore get a passage. In the absence of a proprietary barometer you could make your own by turning an empty whisky bottle neck down into an old jam jar containing about two inches of water. Then, with rising pressure, the water would climb up inside the neck of the bottle. It is uncanny but this really seems to work. It is cheap as well; in those days you could get a good bottle of scotch for a couple of quid and a pot of jam for one shilling and threepence. The only trouble was it kept getting knocked over and broken, and as everything that went wrong in the barge was always the mate's fault, he would then have to buy a new bottle of Scotch, whilst the skipper's contribution would be the pot of jam.

Shell Oil used to have a half page advert in one of the yachting magazines. It consisted of a photograph of the sky showing a different cloud formation each month and explaining what it meant. It went on to say 'but you can always rely on Shell'. I collected the whole series of these advertisements and made them into a book.

I had an ancient publication of the Royal Yacht Squadron, and in it was a recipe for a storm glass. It was supposed to foretell wind only and not be influenced by rain. I told Mick Lungley about this and he got quite excited by it. We were anchored off Southend at the time and so we went ashore on the pier and got the pier train to the shore and walked to the High Street. There we found an old-fashioned chemist's shop, and inside was an elderly pharmacist in charge.

Mick Lungley
at the wheel of
Cranfield's **Venture**.

He smiled when he heard what we wanted and said, "Yes, I made a lot of these for the old fishermen many years ago. Come back in half-an-hour." When we arrived back he had two medicine bottles ready for us and charged us two bob each, with instructions that the cotton wool-like appearance would settle down to a clear liquid if we did not shake them about. Gingerly we returned to our barges and left them to settle down. The next day we hailed each other at the Spitway. "How's your storm glass, Mick?" I shouted. "My bottle appears to have cleared somewhat." "We must be in for a hurricane," he laughed back; "Mine is all bubbling out over onto the deck!"

Chapter XVII

On the Yard

Once every two years, a working barge would need to go on the shipyard for a general refit. This would happen during the summer months and would run into a period of about three weeks. First, the crew would lower the gear down and get the sails into the sailmakers; sometimes they would only need a little work on each, but also if a sail had stretched then it could be recut. The skipper would have a list of the things that he knew needed doing; for instance, he may need a blacksmith to look at the winch handles and make them fit better on the winches. The list that he would hand to the ship's husband would typically include items such as re-leather the pumps; repair the barge boat; repair a leeboard; replace a snatch[9]; re-whelp the windlass and put the barge on the blocks in order to find that elusive little leak. The number of jobs could be many and varied.

The crew, now with the mast down, would set to work cleaning the grease from off the topsail hoops and inside the topmast cap and from around the main mast in way of the collar lashing. With this done they would then set to work scraping the topmast back to clean wood, and applying about four coats of raw linseed oil. Only the heel that formed the doubling would be varnished. If you varnished the part that the topsail hoops rode up you would have been laughed at, yet the yachtsmen did it. The codes of practice were generations old, and only the simple-minded deviated from the norm. The topmast pole is where you could show a bit of independence, and some skippers preferred this to be varnished, or painted white or blue or black. Black really made a gilded truck stand out.

Then the main mast would be scraped back to the bare wood. Three-cornered scrapers were the tool, sharpened up with a file. For this job you needed to start work at about seven in the morning, and if two men kept at it all day it could be scraped and sandpapered by evening. It would then be too late in the day to

9: *Snatch - a fairlead.*

varnish, so a coat of raw linseed oil would be applied to protect it from possible thunderstorms or even a very heavy dew. If the weather was still favourable the next morning, the mast would be rubbed dry with clean cloths and a coat of varnish would be applied; at a later date a second coat would be added.

The servings on the rigging would be overhauled, and made good with a coat of Stockholm tar. The blocks would all be strung up in the hold to be worked on during any rainy days. They would have to be knocked apart, greased, then reassembled and painted, the wooden ones painted mast colour and the metal ones painted in the new-fangled aluminium paint. The old boys said that metal blocks should always be painted black, but if you went back still further then green would have been the colour of choice - but we hotheads knew it all anyway.

We would then spend the day heaving the mast up. I say a day, as in the process we would paint the sprit (pronounced 'spreet') on its way up. As the mainsail was still ashore, a temporary headrope would be rigged in order to hold the sprit aloft.

Once we had collected the sails from the loft we would prepare to dress them. Our dressing was made up of 60lb. yellow ochre placed into a 45 gallon oil drum, followed by 30lbs. red ochre, to which water would be added, stirring constantly. When a tan liquid had been achieved then 8 gallons of cod oil would go in. Much more stirring had to take place in order to form an emulsion, then more water had to go in to nearly fill the drum. Now the magic ingredient would be added, such as stale beer from the local pub. This did add a shine to the sails, which bargemen thought allowed the wind to travel more quickly over their surface. The above is the Francis & Gilders' recipe.

Different firms had a slight variation in colour. These recipes were secret and closely guarded by the various ship's husbands and not disclosed to anyone. Now the secret is out!

10: The bolt rope of a sail is traditionally sewn to the port side of the edge of the canvas. When sails are spread out for dressing, portside up, the bolt rope is accessible for preservation treatment with Stockholm tar.

The sails would be spread in a nearby meadow, port-side up so that the mate could paint Stockholm tar onto the bolt ropes. To make it easier to apply, we would usually warm it up first. This was the time to get out your really old clothes as they would only be fit for chucking away afterwards. The sail dressing would then be

Memory heaving up, her mast freshly varnished, topmast oiled, the windlass paused whilst the sprit is painted.

applied using soft brooms, first one side then turning over for the other side. We would leave them for about three days, spreading them out each day and folding them up at night. We did not leave them too long folded as being wet they were subject to spontaneous combustion.

A few days later we would get a couple of extra hands, if we could, to help us lug the mainsail aboard and lay it in position along the hatches. The mast would be lowered and the sail bent on, at the same time reeving new cordage; lowers and middles, peak brails, etc.

I once asked our ship's husband why we used waterproof sisal for our cordage when I thought manila would have been better. He stood back and looked at me askance, pipe coming out of his mouth. "Jim," he exclaimed, "the guv'nor buys sisal for three very good reasons - first, it's cheap, second, it don't cost very much, and third, it is inexpensive."

121

The mast would be hove up and the topmast raised aloft; sometimes the topsail would have been bent on whilst the mainmast was still lowered down, but much the better way was to stop it up[11] and send it aloft. The mate would then sit on the mainmast head and bend on the hoops as the skipper hauled the sail aloft.

Once the sails were all bent on and rigged they would still be set each fine day to assist the drying, but in fact the dressing never really dried. There was a saying that when the dressing on the sails stopped coming off on your clothes, it was time to dress them again. As the barge was not hauled out of the water we never painted under her bottom, but we did not get any barnacles growing as the Thames water was so polluted they could not survive. However the sides needed a good scrub and when dry we would stop up any spike holes with coal tar putty, which was known as 'boom and teak'. We made this up ourselves using whiting powder with coal tar being added.

The barge would then be given a nice coat of gas-house tar. If it was a cold day we would warm the tar up first, and whilst the tar was still wet we would brush on a coat of plumbago (black lead). This we would mix up ourselves and consisted only of black lead powder and water well stirred together; I always added a good helping of flour which lightened the colour and gave it a bit more body. This mixture was then payed onto the wet tar, all except the wale[12] which was left jet black with the tar. The black lead filled all the little imperfections in the barge's planks and gave for a very smooth surface and indeed a very handsome finish.

The owner by this time would be shouting down the phone, "How much longer are you going to be? We need the barge in London." We, the crew would also be getting fed up, having sweated and reeked of fish oil, grease, paint, tar, linseed oil, and everything else in between, all for a miserly retainer which was 'yard pay'.

With a sigh of relief you let go of the yard ropes and slipped into the tide; the topsail fills, "Drop your mains'l out!" The water chuckles as it runs along the lee side; you have time to take it all in, yes, she really is a lovely thing.

[11]: *Stopping up - the practice of tying a sail with light line into a sausage like bundle before hoisting aloft to bend on. Sometimes weak line was purposely used so that a sail could be 'broken-out' when needed.*
[12]: *Wale - the top plank in a sailing barge's side, usually of thicker timber than those below.*

Chapter XVIII

It wasn't always summer

The year of 1947 was recorded as the coldest winter for thirty years, and 1953 was almost as bad. The winter of 1962/3 was even colder, setting new records when on Boxing Day the temperature fell to below freezing and remained so for three months, making it the coldest winter recorded since 1740.

The rivers froze over, and the army was called in to blow up the ice on the Colne to enable Everard's coal ships to get to the Hythe. Nothing got up to or away from Mistley for over a fortnight.

The barges had all taken advantage of the north-easterlies and managed to get to London to get loaded, but could not make the passage back down the Swin. The Thames and Sheerness anchorages were packed full of barges waiting for a slant in the weather.

The scientists, having finished with the war, could now put their minds to other matters and discovered that the world was getting cooler. 'Global cooling' was in the news and it was rumoured that the world was entering into a new Ice Age. Their findings were so impressive that it caused Friends of the Earth to be formed in 1973. It was calculated that if the earth cooled by three degrees centigrade then a new Ice Age would occur. There was speculation that man would no longer be able to survive on the British Isles and we would all have to migrate to Southern Europe. Against this background of pessimism, we did what we always did and just got on with it.

In the sea, there were patches of ice on the salt water, reinforced with an abundance of snow. The spray hit the beaches and froze into larger and larger lumps, whilst the fresh water in the upper reaches also froze. Snow over the saltings floated off on the big tides, and turned into ice, which choked the tidal estuaries, creeks and rivers. It became so thick that it made all the rivers, and even the Swin, impossible to navigate. Once frozen into such a mass, any boat was carried along with it, backwards and forward with the ebb and flow of the tide. Even boats on a mooring were not safe as the complete mooring was dragged along with the boat, ground chain and anchors together.

Tollesbury when fully rigged.

In the Wallet, the **Cabby** spent three days helplessly drifting with the ebb and flow whilst being frozen into the ice. Alec Rands, her skipper, even found his engine useless, as ice particles blocked the cooling system.

I resorted to sending my mate aloft one bright moonlit night so that he could con me into the black clear water, the moonlight reflecting off the ice and showing it up clearly. On another occasion, when I was in R. & W. Paul's **Tollesbury**, which was fitted with an engine, we ran into such thick ice in the middle of the night that the barge came to a complete stop. We had been running into broken ice for several hours and this could be very damaging. I had hung stack boards over the bow in an attempt to prevent the ice from cutting into the hull.

Once we had run into such a thick mass it soon closed in around us, and I stopped the engine as we were no longer moving. In order to check that the barge was not damaged I lit the paraffin riding light (I had not got a torch) and got out onto the ice. With the light from the lamp I walked all around the barge on the ice checking that her planking was not damaged.

Tollesbury as a motor barge.

Keeping warm under these circumstances was the all-important thing. Modern synthetic materials had not been invented, so two pairs of trousers were the order of the day complete with two jerseys and a jacket. When underway, only an army overcoat, or better still a hooded duffle coat, was all that was available.

I put Gordon Hardy ashore at the Hope Point to get more provisions. He wore two of everything plus a duffle coat with the hood turned up. He had to traipse through three miles of deep snow drifts to get to the village of Cliffe. It took him some three hours, by which time he was covered in frozen snow. Even his beard was covered; as he left the marshes he looked like some huge abominable snowman. The kids were just leaving school for their dinner break as Gordon entered the village, and they all ran screaming back into the school and barricaded themselves in.

It was 'Young Spiro' Ling who showed me how to make the best gloves you could ever get. They were in fact mittens with a thumb, made from an old overcoat. You simply laid your hand on the coat and drew a line around it. With two of these for each hand, they could be sewn together with sail twine to create mittens. They could not be used for heaving up the anchor or setting sail, but for steering, I thought they were an absolute luxury. A poor alternative was an old pair of socks.

Getting enough coal to keep warm was vital; it was our only form of heating. In the '40s and '50s, most power stations were powered by coal, so that the Thames would have thousands of tons of it sitting about in lighters. There was an 'understanding' that bargemen could 'borrow' as much coal as needed, provided it was for your own use. It was good practice to be fairly discreet about this, and we endeavoured to get the coal aboard at quiet times when no one was about.

This did not always go to plan. I was on a coal jetty at Erith, and took the barge boat on the inside of the jetty to be less noticeable. All went well, and we had loaded the boat with the best Welsh black diamonds when I discovered that the boat was aground. My dismay grew even deeper as a police boat came cruising slowly up the river, shining their searchlight under all of the jetties. Of course, he spotted our boat aground and called out, "Are you alright sailorman?" He knew that we were from the sailing barge at anchor as there was no boat astern of her. "We're okay," I shouted back; "I have just been ashore for the phone and my mate has got the boat grounded." "Hang on," called the Bobby, "We'll pull you off." True to his word, he edged in and we threw him the boat's painter. He gently backed out from under the jetty, dragging us through the slimy mud and into deep water. Our boat sank deeper and deeper into the water with us sitting on the coal, deeply embarrassed and dreading the boat foundering under the weight of our 'illicit' cargo.

Fortunately we remained afloat and, as the police boat dropped us off back at our barge, the Bobby shouted, "Don't be so bloody greedy next time!" His laugh as he motored off told us we could relax and enjoy our ill-gotten gains to keep warm in peace.

Chapter XIX

Wiffling

We all had a gun on board in the hope of supplementing our food for the pot. This was known as 'wiffling'. It was also a sport, as well as a commercial activity. Fagbury Marshes[13] was a lucrative spot to bag a nice fat hare, as were the marshes below Cliffe. At Shore Ends, just in the River Crouch, we would take the barge boat close under the sea wall and wait for the evening flight of duck.

The guns we owned were a varied and motley collection, more dangerous to the owner than the duck. Mine was a twelve bore shotgun which Mick Lungley found in a junk shop in Ipswich. He had to pay two pounds, ten shillings, for it. It was so slack between the breech and the barrel that each time I fired it I got a face full of oil.

I was out shooting with Mick one day when the contraption fired off on its own accord and Mick felt the blast from it. That night, whilst laying in my bunk, I was so worried that I turned out and chucked it overboard and then slept more easily.

I once co-owned a punt gun with fellow barge skipper Peter Light, which we had bought off Mona Clark, the landlady of 'The Jolly Sailor' pub at Heybridge Basin, near Maldon. Peter had his own punt, so we pooled our resources to good effect, though I suspect the ducks were hardly quaking in their boots. Whilst Peter settled the financial account with Mona, I went round to the back shed to fetch the gun, all ten feet of it, and as much as I could carry. As I leaned it up against the front wall of 'The Jolly Sailor', Mona let us know that the gun was loaded. This was because it was a muzzle-loaded weapon, which if not fired due to lack of suitable targets, could not be easily unloaded, as one could remove a cartridge, and would have to be left loaded for the next occasion.

I had the license for the black powder, which I bought from Radcliffe's in Colchester High Street. Taking the bus to Maldon,

13: *Fagbury Marshes border the north shore of the River Orwell west of Felixstowe. They later disappeared under concrete with the expansion of Felixstowe Container port complex.*

A punt gun and punt of the open Essex type, belonging to Walter Linnett of Bradwell, one of the last men to work a duck punt for a living.

I would ride on the top deck where I was able to have a smoke, the black powder in a carrier bag besides me!

Alf Drake of Mersea had an old muzzle-loading eight bore shot gun. He kept the shot in one pocket of his jacket and the black powder in the other. One day he absentmindedly put his lit pipe in the wrong pocket. He survived to tell the tale and learn a lesson; luckily just blowing out the side of his jacket!

The interior of the High Street, Colchester, premises of K.D. Radcliffe, gunmakers, founded in 1787 and still in business in 2018.

Chapter XX

A Winter's Tale

The life of a sailing barge skipper, especially in the winter time, was always one of uncertainty, without today's forecasting technology to help him keep out of trouble. Vigilance was the name of the game - when to go and when to stop. On that judgement of the weather depended the opportunity to make a decent living for himself and the mate as well as show a profit for the owner.

Let me illustrate this by inviting you to join me on a trip I made in the **Memory**. If you grab an extra jersey you can imagine that you are on board.

We are at Ipswich, and have just unloaded wheat at Cranfield's flour mill, and pulled over to an empty berth by the dockers' canteen. This is a Monday, and by the time we are covered up and have got the barge ready for sea, it is late afternoon. I just have time to call in at the Ipswich Steamship Office and get Margaret to ring the Mistley office for me. Our orders are as I expected, 'London Light', and as is the normal practice, rather than wasting time going to Mistley to square up, I draw a £25 sub from Margaret and say that I expect to leave on tomorrow's day tide.

During the Monday night there is a heavy fall of snow, and by dawn it is frozen. Luckily we have taken in fresh water the afternoon before, as the fresh water standpipe is now frozen solid. Tuesday morning sees us clearing all the solid snow off the decks and checking that the anchor chain is not frozen to the windlass. It is, and we have to have a kettle of boiling water poured on it to release it from the wooden windlass barrel. Likewise, the bowlines in our big shore ropes have to have the same treatment before they will yield to our efforts to untie them. The only reason that the dock itself is not frozen over is because of pollution by chemicals which are known to be in the waters around here.

Snow and ice need to be cleared from the barge as frozen ropes and slippery decks would be a recipe for trouble.

Now we have cleared the barge of the worst of the snow, we can go out and buy ourselves a huge kitbag of grub. We will also call at Whitmore's, the sailmakers, for ten gallons of paraffin oil. This is for our lamps and of course the faithful Primus stove.

The tide at Ipswich is at 1.30 p.m., but first we have to get down the dock to the lock. The tugs at Ipswich have all packed up since the decline of the sailing barges, so we have no choice but to sail or heave. One of Mick's pals has come on board to give us a hand as far as the lock gates. From our berth at the top of the dock we will hold her on slip ropes whilst we set the sails and lower both leeboards, and with a light southerly wind, we can sail from our berth. Ipswich Dock is L-shaped, and at the corner we can sail close-hauled, and make several boards down the dock, with the mate standing by the foresail halliards, as each time we tack she might be shy of coming through the wind.

We know our barge very well, and time the last tack to come up head to wind and nudge her onto the inner pier head and catch a turn with our rope on the bollard ashore. The lock at Ipswich is about 400ft long, and it is usual to wait for a level, that is, when the water on the outside of the dock is the same level as the inside. This is when both inner and outer gates are open at the same time.

Ipswich Lock was well manned in the '50s; five men to each side, and with the wind straight in we need an offing. The gallant lock-gate men hand us a hemp heaving line, from each side of the lock, which we make fast to either side of our fore horse. With our sails pinned in, the ten men heave away on the heaving lines, and soon break into a fair trot. By the time that we shoot out of the lock at the other end, we have plenty of way on to bear away on the port tack and start our slow turn to windward down along Cliff Quay.

We are down by the power station by the time we begin to feel a little help from the ebb tide. "Time to put the kettle on, Mick." The wind, if blowing up one reach, will be up every reach, so it is turn, turn, turn, all the way down the river. By the time we reached the Stone Heaps at Shotley, I think we have had enough and anchor with 15 fathoms of chain. The light is failing and we have just saved putting the nav' lights in. While the mate puts up the riding light, I nip below to get the five to six shipping forecast. It is not bad, with S.W. 4-5 in Thames, and 4 in Dover. Ah well, we can expect a long turn to windward but we should be able to have a go.

The polished cabin looks very cosy in the lamplight. We've got a good fire going, and we soon build up a lovely glow. With a bit of grub on, I then consult the tide table. It is going to be low water at 8.30 a.m. and so I tell Mick we muster about 5 a.m. in the morning. We both turn in early, but I look out several times in the night to see that the weather is holding up.

It is Wednesday morning, and I turn out about 4.30 a.m. and put the kettle on. We heave up the anchor, and with the nav' lights in we carry the ebb out of the harbour. On the pitch of the Naze, we unship the nav' lights as daylight appears. Dawn always seems to be the coldest part of the day, and I nip below and put another jersey on. I notice that the flood has already started. "Blast." I wish that I had mustered an hour sooner; but then, we always wish we'd started an hour earlier.

I revel in the smell of eggs and bacon coming from the cabin hatch - lovely! I will let Mick have his breakfast first and then go down for mine, finishing with my favourite, fried bread and apricot jam all washed down with a mug of tea. With another mug to take up on deck, I call, "'Bout oh, Mick." and she comes round with a flurry of canvas. With mainsail, topsail, foresail, mizzen and jib we carry

Memory at dusk
works to
windward in an
empty river.

132

the best part of 3,000 sq. ft. of canvas. We lay across the Spitway and over the Whittaker Spit. "Time to put the kettle on, Mick."

With a long and short board up the Swin, at the Maplin Spit she looks like fetching up; time to get a bit of grub on. At the Blacktail Spit the wind is starting to draw down. Well, that's what the forecast gave anyway. We've done well so far. I give her a good leg to windward then put her round again to fetch Southend Pier, with the flood tide nearly done. Another tack over to the Kent shore, then wind round once more and hang well up to windward.

We bring up at the East Blyth and lay anchored for the ebb tide. At slack water, that is 9 p.m. that night, we put the side lights in and get underway. The night is clear but cold with the wind moderate from the west - sou'- west. I only intend going as far as 'The Ship and Lobster' at Denton, Gravesend, so that I can phone the London office in the morning.

That's me, Jim, by the wheel, Mick Alexander on the companion steps, the photo taken by a guest aboard who accepted my invitation!

The night-time river is so quiet, hardly another vessel underway, the strong Thames tide pushes the barge well to windward of her course as she tacks back and forth from Kent to Essex, and we gain much ground to windward. As we near the barge anchorage at 'The Ship and Lobster' I shout, "Mick, I think we will try Erith." He is not surprised as we have done this before. On we go. I know how busy the river will be on the day tide, but tonight we have it all to ourselves. The pungent smells seem to lure you on. Hedley's, the soap works, smells like a French boudoir. In Long Reach there is the sewage works, and every other smell that you could think of. As we approach Erith, Mick is half expecting my next comment. "You know, Mick, I think it would be just as well, as we are underway, to go up to Woolwich Buoys. How about a cup of tea?"

As we approach the Woolwich Buoys the drill is to tack just above the buoy, and then get the mainsail off as we wind for the last time. Bringing her head round will enable us to use the tide as a brake, taking sail off as we go, so that we are just making way over the tide.

Tonight no other barges are moored here, so we will have to get a slip rope through the ring of the buoy. Mick is good at this and we meet with no trouble. Once the barge is moored we can then shackle our wire on the buoy and make this fast to our windlass. The time is now 2 a.m. Thursday.

When work is slack, other barges will be moored here, making coming alongside and mooring up much easier. However, being the only barge here on this occasion means that we will be first on turn for a freight.

At 10 a.m. I go ashore in the boat and ring the London office. They tell me that there is nothing doing at the moment and to ring back in the afternoon. This is a normal occurrence, but as soon as I get back on board, Mrs. Riley from the nearby tug office hails me and asks me to get back on the telephone immediately. She always gets a nice present from the firm for running these errands. When I ring the office, Jimmy Heywood, our London broker says, 155 tons of maize for Mistley. I tell him that 155 tons is too much for Memory but he says that the parcel has got to be cleared. As it is the only freight on offer I decide to accept the responsibility, and know that the barge will have a large stack in the hatchway and, that being deep, she will sail like a pig.

We get underway immediately with the wind straight down, which means tacking up the river to the Surrey Commercial Dock. This is how I wanted it to be, since once loaded it will be a fair wind home. The Thames on a daytime flood is much different from a quiet night sail like last night, when we had the river to ourselves. You can understand now why I persisted in keeping underway until 2 a.m.

Today the river is full of craft, tugs towing six lighters at a time, blowing four and two or four and one blasts when turning head to tide either to port or starboard, to release their charges or to pick up additional craft. Tankers, 'flat iron' colliers, Baltic timber ships, all are rushing up river to save this precious flood tide, which in effect is worth thousands of horsepower in itself. There are workboats and police launches scurrying this way and that to add to the excitement. Then there are coasters getting off their berths and slowly punching the tide down the river in order to get to their continental port of loading for tomorrow's work.

The 'Flat-Iron' collier **Brimsdown**. A fine bone in her teeth, she has minimum air-draft with folding funnel and masts for going 'above bridges' in the London River.

Through this maze of craft we have to tack our barge. There is no question of power giving way to sail; all they can do is hold their course, and we will have to duck and dive. We will make a short one here, under the stern of that one there, trusting that everyone knows their job and trusts us as we trust them; it is only rarely that things go wrong.

Once off the Surrey Dock entrance, we tack just above the lock and get the sail off, using the tide to check us onto the pier head and catch a turn.

It is all hell at the Surrey Dock. Once there, you live with a fender in each hand as lighters shoot off tugs and bang alongside. It is the swim heads that do the most damage, as they tend to ride up over your rails; with a boathook you can sometimes sheer it round so that it will fall flat alongside. The only way you can get any peace is to moor a drifting lighter alongside and use that as a fender. Eventually we lock in, and our ship is the Cunard freighter at the top of the Greenland Dock, port side.

Inside the dock is complete chaos with all the 'drifters' piled up along the lock gates. Everything we run our dolly line[14] to wants to heave to us, rather than allow us to heave to it. Eventually we fight our way through and up to our berth; still just as much of a jungle, but at least the grain elevator is alongside, so we can hope for a quick shoot tomorrow. At 5 p.m. the dock goes quiet, and while we are having our supper we wonder how it can all work, it seems so

[14] *Dolly line - a long flexible wire wound on a barrel mounted on the windlass bitt heads, mostly used to heave a barge around the docks, where sailing was banned.*

John Impey fends off a swim-headed lighter intent on inflicting damage to the **Memory**.

The melee that was Docklands; an ancient steamer forces a passage, whilst a sailorman, right of picture, tries to keep out of trouble.

totally disorganised. On Friday, at 8 a.m., I am on board to see the ship worker. "'Ang on where y'are, sailorman. We'll give you a shout just after mobile." All bargemen are called sailormen in the docks, as a distinct contrast to their own lightermen; 'after mobile' means after their tea break, which is about 10.30 a.m.

It takes about 40 minutes to load 155 tons of grain. As soon as we are called, we heave alongside the floating elevator having previously taken off all the hatches. When the golden grain runs into the hold the mate and I are in there with shovels trimming the side decks and 'cupboard'[15] aft. The dust rises as thick as fog, dry choking dust that gets in the eyes and up your nose. We really should have worn masks; but we did not even think of it.

With a "That's yer lot, sailorman!" we are shoved out, as another empty lighter is shoved in to take our place. We find the quietest spot nearby to catch a turn, and go up and get our pass, stating

A dock pass, certifying that we are loaded and what with. This would normally be handed in at the lock when leaving the dock; however, this particular pass was issued at Bellamy's Wharf, on the river outside the Surrey Docks, so was kept.

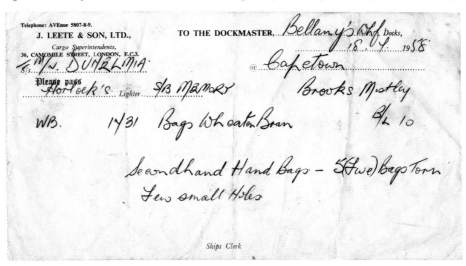

that we are loaded and with what. We lose a further half-hour for the Customs to stamp our pass. We hurry back on board before the barge gets broken up in the melee that is dockland.

Right, let's get out of this. Shove her clear. There is a little draught down the dock, so we set the topsail to save heaving. The skipper of a P.L.A. tug calls through his hailer, "Oi, sailorman, you are not allowed to $%@#ing sail in the $%@#ing dock." I shout back, "I'm not $%@#ing sailing, I am $%@#ing drifting!" "What's that $%@#ing sail doing then?" I reply, "I'm $%@#ing drying it!" Nothing else is said but he has got rid of the bile in his stomach.

[15] Cupboards - in this context the under-deck hold space up to the aft bulkhead. If the cupboards are not filled or 'trimmed' the cargo may shift with risks to a vessels safety.

The floating grain elevator in the dock used to fill lighters, sailing barges, motor barges and small coasters with cereals, commonly wheat.

He rings down full ahead on the bridge telegraph and charges up the dock. These Cockneys really can swear; I think it was them that taught us bargemen.

Just then the wind drops, and a few minutes later the flag lazily lifts, but straight up the dock. "Oh, no – not easterly." Now it is my turn to swear. In a miserable mood, we drop the topsail and heave the rest of the way down the dock. We find a quiet place by the lock, comparatively quiet that is, and moor a drifter alongside of us and cover up.

There is a lock-out soon after 4 p.m. and we hang onto a tug and lighter and get a snatch out. The sooner we are out of this hell-hole the better. High water at London Bridge is at 4.17 p.m., so the tide is well away by the time we get clear of the lock. As we tack down the river it seems 'a miserable look on', with hardly enough wind to keep her sailing.

Ready to lock-out at the Greenland entrance, Surrey Docks. The **Leofleda**'s skipper, Buff Chittick, has made sure his ropes on the hatchcloths are neetly coiled, a tidy contrast to the general chaos of the docks.

You can see the white water under the swims of the moored lighters that line both sides of the river as the ebb roars down. It is an exacting job making sure that you use the full width of the river yet tacking in good time so as not to get caught under those murderous swims. It then starts to rain to complete our ecstasy. We ship our nav' lights in Gallions Reach; at least the river is wider here and there is a little more wind with a bit of south in it. Ah well, we have had enough of it at Erith and go in and anchor, taking the side lights out and putting the riding light up before going below. We hope the wind will go southerly tomorrow, or are we in for an easterly spell?

With high water in London at 4.38 a.m., we muster at 5 with the wind in the south-east, a nice sailing breeze about Force four, and fetch away. We make two tacks in Long Reach, run down Halfway Reach, and harden up to turn down Northfleet Hope, making the East Blyth by low water where we bring up. It is a strange quirk of mine that if I use the East Blyth anchorage, I always go above the buoy when I am bound up and anchor below the buoy when I am bound down.

The afternoon high water is about 4.30 p.m. with a flat calm, oily swell and drizzly rain. Visibility is poor and so it will be bad after dark. I decide not to go, and lay that ebb at anchor. We give the wedges an extra knock in, gripe[16] down spars and ropes on the hatches, pull the boat up in the davits and gripe it well in.

Before going below I see a skein of black-bellied geese fly in. They have flown all the way from Russia, a sure sign of bad weather and without a doubt from the north-east. The five to six forecast on the radio does not offer much hope either, north-easterly in Humber and German Bight, but south-easterly in Thames and Dover. Well, we can but try.

By Sunday morning, 4 a.m., the wind is south-sou-east about Force four, and the lights ashore are twinkling and very bright. Not a good sign. I think the wind will come easterly. Well, the glass is beginning to rise; shall we have a go? Yes, come on, we might make the Colne, or if it lays on we can run back to Sheerness. Getting underway, it's bloody cold; we can only just fetch our course.

We have not been underway for long when the wind falls light and, sure enough, begins to back, with drizzly rain which then turns to sleet. This isn't much of a look on, because loaded deep as the **Memory** is, we only make low water at the Maplin Spit. We anchor for the flood tide when a lumpy swell begins to roll in. I know what this means. Sure enough, a little draught of air picks up from the east, and as soon as there is enough wind to make way over the tide I get under weigh.

The **Memory**'s decks get full and fuller as the swell picks up with more wind. We could still run back for Sheerness, but let's try and get through the Spitway; we will then have Colne under our lee. It is dark again by the Whitaker so ship the lights once more. As we bear away for the Spitway, it is an hour and a half to low water. We can't get down the Wallet in that time… but come on, let's have a go. Once through, luff up hard; we don't have to haul the sheets in as we have not slacked off for the Spitway, so perhaps I knew in my mind that we were going to keep trying for Harwich.

The trouble is, once you take shelter, you will be holed up for a week, or quite a bit longer. The wind is heading us; it is nearly a dead punch. Ah well, plug on while we can. By Hollands Low[17] we can see that the tide is flooding; tack off towards the Gunfleet again. With Mick on the lead, I shout, "Soon as you get a bottom, Mick, then 'bout-oh; we don't want to risk breaking a leeboard."

16. *Gripe - in this context, to tighten a rope lashing to make it secure, or add additional ropes to loose gear or the barge's boat in anticipation of heavy weather.*
17. *Holland's Low - A part of the Essex coast off Holland Gap, where once a small river joined the North Sea.*

Nearly every swell will wash the deck of a deep-laden barge. Here the Medusa buoy is a speck on the horizon under a leaden sky, as the barge nears the lower end of the Wallet channel, bound for Harwich Haven.

Soon, back on the starboard tack, I said, "Try the pump Mick." I have great faith in the **Memory**, she's a strong barge, but with the amount of sea and wind, she might be straining. Mick ships the pump, and normally would have to prime it with a bucket of water, but not tonight - all he has to do is wait for a big wave to come along the deck which fills the pump hole and away he goes. The pump is bringing up solid water, and I am a bit concerned about how much might be in the bilge. I don't want to wet the cargo. Just then a rogue wave came over the weather quarterboard and washed down through the steerage, knocking Mick off his feet and leaving him lying in the scuppers. He simply picked himself up and started pumping again. I take no notice, as I am more concerned with the water coming out of the pump. I say, "Here Mick, catch hold of her and let me have a go," but after a few minutes, air comes hissing up with the water and I know that the bilge is dry. I am relieved; that is a weight off my mind.

A deep-loaded barge can be a wet ship in a breeze of wind. I unship the pump and stow it under the steering box aft, and before putting the heavy cast iron tomkin[18] back on the pump hole, I roll a malt sack, which we normally use as a mat under the wheel, and shove it tightly down the pump shaft. Barges have been lost by ingress of water through the pump hole before. "'Bout oh, Mick," and around we go once more.

Once on the new tack with the weather leeboard up, I say, "Right, Mick, go and get yourself changed." Mick says, "I've got nothing else to change into, Jim, everything else is soaking wet." "Right," says I, "raid my lockers and take what you want from them." Soon, I hear the comforting sound of the fire being made up; at least it's warm down there. Mick hands me up a steaming hot mug of Oxo, just the thing for washing the tannin out of your mouth after so many cups of tea.

Time to tack again. Taking bearings, I think that next time on the starboard tack we will fetch round the Naze, but each time the Naze remains stubbornly off the starboard bow, and we make many more tacks. It is a long night, but eventually the tide eases and we make better way in spite of a large swell. At last we clear the Naze and I tell Mick to have a lie-down on the locker.

With the coming of daylight we roar into Harwich, and on the Guard, I nip down to give Mick a shake. I can't help smiling to myself, as laying there in his wet clothes steam is rising off him with the heat from the cabin. With the wind free we run into the Stour and anchor off Wrabness. It will be another six hours before we can sail up to Mistley, and it is going to be a fair wind anyway. The weather can do what it likes now.

We go below; the kettle is singing on the hob. Right! Let's have that frying pan on, double eggs and bacon, and shove four of those sausages in for good measure. Ah, that's better; now for a kip on the locker. We can't turn-in properly as we will be getting underway soon and can't afford to oversleep.

Sailing up to Mistley is easy enough; after all it is our home port. Topsail, mainsail slacked out to the sprit and the foresail is all we want. Just before we reach the mill, I shove the helm hard over to starboard and let her forefoot ground onto the high mud bank. As her head comes off we touch the anchor down and let her drudge alongside into the berth. It is snowing again, but let it - we're home!

[18]. *Tomkin - the cast iron cover that locates over the bilge pump deck opening. It is heavy, curved on top to allow free flow of water over it and often secured by a short chain to an eyebolt in the deck in case it is unshipped accidentally.*

Chapter XXI

Unloading at Yarmouth

As more and more of the auxiliary motor barges had their sailing gear taken out, the sailing barge once again came into its own, as the method of unloading at Yarmouth used a 'gin wheel'.

To rig a gin wheel, the topsail halliard and topsail sheet were unshackled from the sail, and the gin wheel would then be slung between them, allowing the gin wheel to traverse the whole of the main hold. A wire would be led through the gin wheel to a dolly winch which would straddle the main horse and be wedged tightly into position. The winch, which was supplied by the mill, would have two handles so that a man could heave from either side. The other end of the wire would have a piece of chain to act as a counterweight, so that it would not run up and out of the gin wheel. At the bitter end of the chain would be a large steel ring with which to make a 'snotter' (lasso) to raise the sacks out of the hold.

A gin wheel.

Gin wheels were rigged to discharge cargo from barge's holds. This drawing shows a set up which served the length and breadth of the main hatch opening. For the forehold the gin wheel might be set up on the staysail halliard.

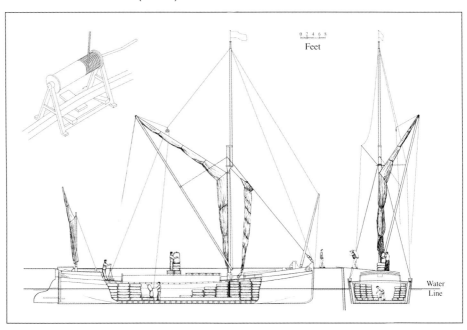

A pair of hatches were placed in position across the hold, with more hatches piled on top until they reached the same height as the

Memory at Gt. Yarmouth, eager to leave her berth on Bunn's wharf, where her gin wheel would have been used to discharge her cargo.

quay. Two planks would then be laid across from the quay and onto the raised hatches, forming the roadway on which a man could walk. In order that the man could take a sack onto his back, a platform of sacks (part of the cargo) would be built on to the hatches onto which the winched-up sack would be landed.

It was one man's job to remain on the stage to receive the sack, remove the chain from the neck of it, and send the chain back down into the hold. He kept the sack in an upright position until the porter had got it on to his back. As he walked off, another man would come along the dual plank, just as a further sack would be coming up. With two men on the winch handles, one man in the hold hooking on, another man on the stage to receive the sacks plus three or four men portering the sacks into the mill, it meant that you needed a gang of seven to eight men to unload a barge. With a cargo of sixteen or seventeen hundred bags, it would take two days of dusty hard work to empty her hold.

On one occasion after unloading, the wind remained stubbornly from the east and blew very hard. On the third day it lessened a bit, but was still too much for us. However I did inform the tug skipper

By the mid-1950s a sailing barge was becoming a rarity around the coast. This is **Memory** on 21st March 1957, after unloading at Gt. Yarmouth.

that I was ready to sail and I was just waiting for a little more improvement in the weather. After a hard easterly blow, you normally reckoned on allowing a further twenty-four hours in order to let the swell die down, but by that evening it fell to almost a calm and remained so all night.

Next morning there was a good sailing breeze again. I thought my chances looked good, so I took the first bus to Gorleston and stood on the pier head for a good fifteen minutes studying the sea. Yes, I thought, I could manage with this. The wind being straight in the Haven, I definitely needed the tug of course. Now my mind was made up I sprinted back to Gorleston Town Quay, where the tug was moored.

Richard Lee Barber was a foot shorter and the same width as the **Memory**, but dwarfed us nevertheless!

The **Richard Lee Barber** was the Commissioner's general harbour tug, and also a salvage tug. She was steam driven, producing 1500 h.p., and was much the same size as the barge herself in length and breadth. Thankfully she was well subsidised, and the charges for harbour use were very reasonable. I now needed to get on with things, as I wanted the whole of the flood tide to be in my favour.

I called out to the mate of the tug. He looked surprised and told me that the skipper had gone for a haircut. I ran up to the barber's shop, and the skipper was the next to go in the chair. When I told him I wanted to put to sea, he simply said, "Oh - I didn't think that you would want to go today, skip, as you have not got a wheelhouse." To me that seemed quite strange, and then I realised that the other regular sailorman down there was the **Cambria** and she had her whaleback wheelhouse. "No, skip," I replied, "If you can get me well off the shore, I can make a fair wind of this." That good man was a true seaman; he simply put his newspaper down, relinquished his turn and said "You git back to your barge and I'll be up directly."

We soon had the barge griped down, boat up in the davits, rolling wangs[19] set up, and were just lying on slip ropes when the tug appeared. I hadn't got a regular Yarmouth tow rope and offered him, as usual, two of my best mooring ropes. A 'Yarmouth' tow rope is a larger diameter than anything we'd normally carry on board, and was kept for towing through the Yarmouth piers; it was made up specifically for this or any other similar heavy towing work.

The helpful master and crew of the **Richard Lee Barber**.

The tug skipper looked at my mooring ropes and said, "I don't think they will do today, skip, I am going to put you on my rope." This was the big seven inch circumference salvage tow rope. It looked a bit forbidding, all wormed and parcelled up against chafe. The price when you took this rope on was enormous, and I said, "No, I can't take that, skip, it would be cheaper to have another day windbound." The tug skipper said that he wasn't going to book it and nobody would know.

As I took this huge rope, I passed it first around the windlass and then onto the bitt head. I wondered perhaps if I had misjudged the weather. No, I thought, I had taken great care when standing on the pier head and trusted my decision to go.

The tug pulled away. It seemed to be a long way ahead of the barge before the tow rope took the weight and the barge gently followed behind. Even then, the bight of the huge rope did not lift out of the water, and we were soon travelling about the speed of five knots. I was conscious of how quiet it was. The tug at that speed was just ticking over and hardly disturbed the water, and the barge, quite docile, followed obediently behind. It all felt so very smooth, and was a sensation I can still remember.

We slid effortlessly down the Yare, when presently I saw ahead of us a motor barge moored to the quay. She was light, and I should have

[19] *Rolling vangs - two wires from the sprit end, each to a tackle which is hooked to rail eyes forward and tensioned to control the sprit in rough weather; also used in light airs when running before the wind to keep the sprit squared off.*

147

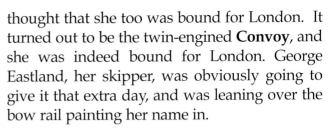

The twin-engined, ex. sailorman, **Convoy**.

thought that she too was bound for London. It turned out to be the twin-engined **Convoy**, and she was indeed bound for London. George Eastland, her skipper, was obviously going to give it that extra day, and was leaning over the bow rail painting her name in.

Suddenly looking up, he saw the **Memory** being towed past. George dropped his paint brush overboard and ran off to start his engines. No way was he going to be left by a sailing barge! This, however, did not induce any sense of bravado in me. I had a very healthy respect for George Eastland's experience, and wondered what sort of a fool am I being towed to sea at the end of a salvage rope. Have I judged the weather correctly? I soon had something else to think about. As we rounded the bend at the mouth of the Haven, I saw the tug rise up on a huge swell, and as the water left her I could see the mass of red antifouling on her bottom. Look out, I thought, it's our turn next, but the tug did not lessen her stride and pulled us through those swells with no effort.

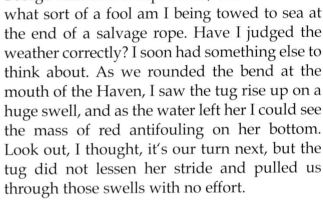

Once outside the Haven, it was less rough, but I needed a good offing and wanted the tug to pull me far to windward. When he thought he had got me well clear he indicated to let go of the rope, but I waved my arms to him to tow me further seaward. This he did, but on the second time he eased down, the rope went right slack and I cast off and bore away on the port tack. The tug crew gave us a friendly wave, even though we had given them a much longer job than expected. Once under the draw of our own sails it was comfortable enough. The swell running in our direction simply lifted the **Memory**'s stern and hurried her on her way.

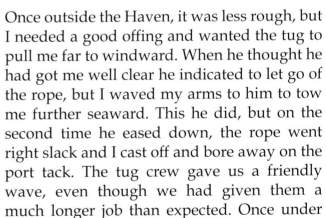

On another occasion **Memory**, loaded with 70 tons of malt for London, stands in to the Shotley anchorage for shelter, where we will bring up to await better weather.

I was surprised to see the coasters, as they punched their way down north, actually going down bows level in the seas. Off Lowestoft, the wind headed us and we had to harden the sheets right in and, once

148

in the Stamford Channel, I thought I needed more sea room and decided to make a tack. Having passed through this difficult little bit we were away again and soon slacked the sheets away once more. Astern we could see the **Convoy** coming along, but I think that the **Memory** was the more comfortable ship. Only after we had passed the Cork lightvessel did the **Convoy**, much further inshore, overtake us. We gave each other a wave as she slowly passed.

We were bound for London, but Harwich loomed invitingly to leeward and proved too much of a temptation. Well, we had done enough for one day, so I bore away and gybed over and made for the harbour. We

found it quiet enough on the Guard and we made our anchorage there. Down below, we were just in time for The Archers, stew and Norfolk dumplings for supper. My last thoughts for the day was that this is much better than a night out at sea and we should be away by about six in the morning.

'Hope this wind holds.' was uppermost in my mind that evening, but deeper down I was also aware that the days of the trading barge was nearing its end.

Memory's cosy cabin with hot tea, good grub, and The Archers was preferable to a night in the open. Hope this wind holds.

The **Geoffrey Stanley**.

With the death of Eastwood's chairman, Mr. Miller, that company lost all interest in the **Memory**, and the talk was all for winding up the trust. Cranfields stopped trading their last two sailormen, **May** and **Spinaway C** about this time, also R. & W. Paul's sold off **Marjorie** and **Anglia**. I could see that the end was nigh, and I took up an offer from H.R. Mitchell to take their motor vessel **Geoffrey**

Stanley, a small, hundred ton, motor ship carrying H.M. Government stores and ammunition.

Peter Light left the **May** to take my place in the **Memory**, but didn't stay long, then John Fairbrother saw her through to the bitter end. These must have been sad days, and he had the task of laying **Memory** up semi-permanently at Lower Halstow. Gradually we each took up different ways of earning our livings. Some of us had several changes before finding something we

It was early 1960; the **Memory**, under skipper John Fairbrother, sets off from Ipswich for laying up at Lower Halstow, Kent, the trust established to keep a working sailing barge in commission having run out of support.

could stick at. John Fairbrother tried his hand at stone masonry, first at Gloucester, then at Canterbury; Peter Light fitted out the smack **Sallie** and took her in continental charter work. Pat Fisher became a docker, but was constantly in demand as a racing skipper, at which he was very successful, and freely passed on his knowledge to anyone who wanted to learn.

Mick Lungley, after coming out of the ex. sailorman **Beric**, spent time in command of Home Trade coasters, in particular the Dutch-built **Rito** in the Baltic timber trade, before stepping ashore. After time as a crane driver at Ransomes, during which he operated the ex. Wisbech Pilot Cutter **Penelope** doing fishing charters, he became a publican, and very successful he was too. Initially he was at The Angel in Woodbridge before buying The Limeburners at Offton, near Ipswich. A pity Mick never got The Butt & Oyster at Pin Mill - it would have been the most perfect combination. Mick also spent 25 years as the Officer of the Day at the Pin Mill Barge Match.

Chapter XXII

Memory finds her way up the tortuous gutway to Saltcote Mill at Mill Beach, on the Blackwater, her home for her new role.

Chartering

The year 1961 saw the Sailing Barge Preservation Society fold; the **Memory** laid-up unrigged at Lower Halstow. The outgoing committee in their wisdom decided that she should be offered for sale by secret bid, and that the total sum that the barge attracted should go to the H.M.S. **Foudroyant**, since then returned back to her original name of **Trincomalee**, which was being preserved at Hartlepool.

They decided that the lowest they would accept would be £350, and so the barge was offered on the market. John Kemp, with the benefit of inside information, decided with a friend of his, Brian Beer, that they would put in a bid of £500. I think this was very fair, as they knew what would be the lowest acceptable bid; other parties did put in bids but each one considerably lower than the £500 offered by John Kemp. There was much criticism of John being successful, but in all fairness to him, he had made the highest bid.

And so **Memory** rigged out again and was returned to Mill

Memory is a very fond memory of mine. Here she is in a smart breeze, everything set, under the Kemp & Beer flag in 1965.

Beach, where she flew the Maldon 'town flag' of blue-white-blue stripes defaced with the letters K&B.

The Barge Club (Thames Barge Sailing Club) had been formed in 1948 with their first barge the **Spurgeon**, allowing the club members to sail using an old retired trading skipper in charge. However, it was a private club, so you could say that John Kemp invented barge chartering, which was to become the future work of the sailing barge. Where would the barge find this work? Foremost in producing the charter parties was a man called Sid Budd; he worked for London Transport but looked more like the original skipper of the **Cutty Sark**. Nevertheless he did produce people, and as the **Memory** hadn't got a regular skipper, the work was shared out amongst John Kemp, Peter Light and myself. Provided a skipper was available, the barge could be used for weeks, weekends and day chartering.

She was very primitive down below; it was Elsan toilets, and hammocks, with a canvas partition to separate the sexes. With Sid's energies in the London area she soon became popular, mainly with students, and besides this we began to collect numerous odd-bods whom Sid described as the 'permanent staff'. Sid would request a financial grant from John Kemp in order to build the barge a store in the fore hold, which soon became a cabin for one of the 'permanent staff'; the fore hold became a rabbit warren of private cabins.

Although Sid did a good job, if the weather was rough, he would come aft and request that the charter fee be lowered as they hadn't had good weather. Another means of getting a rebate would be if they were students; likewise, elderly 'Derby and Joans' also qualified. If you played your cards right you could get a weekend's sailing for as little as ten bob a day. The 'permanent staff' of course came free of charge anyway, and their requirements seemed to come before any other person on board. It was they who dictated the sailing times, which meant sitting in a pub all night, one of the youngest members being sent off to the fish and chip shop, and not returning on board 'til after closing time. The fish and chips were by this time totally cold, but Sid would shove them in the oven. This usually proved disastrous as the paper would catch fire!

Alternatively, if they cooked on board, it would prove just as much a disaster as the cupboard in which all the tinned provisions were kept leaked like a sieve. The tins would all go rusty and the paper labels got washed off, so invariably when making a meal they didn't know what the contents of a tin might be; whether it was chunky meat or sweet Australian pears, once opened it all had to go in together. The mess that resulted was known as 'Goldhanger Goulash' . Les, one of the 'permanent staff', once remarked, "Sid, your grub - t'aint fit fer you'man be-ans!"

I was due to take the **Memory** out one such weekend; she was laying at Mill Beach, way out on the mud. It was going to be high water about 1 a.m.; I arrived in the evening to greet the charterers, and advised them to settle in at the Mill Beach Hotel for a few drinks. I explained that it would be 10 p.m. before we could get them on board. It was during the evening that John Kemp informed me that **Memory**'s port leeboard was laying up at Maldon having been repaired; it was lying in the mud off the shipyard, and John said that he had got slip-ropes under it. With that, he disappeared off home and left me to it. Having got the charterers on board, I left Pauline to get them settled, and to see to the paraffin lights etcetera, whilst I set off in the barge boat to fetch the leeboard with two of the 'permanent staff'.

The charter parties aboard **Memory** were many and varied. This gathering from the prestigious London College of Music have a variety of interpretations of the barging dress code!

A traditional barge leeboard is made of three inch thick oak and held together with heavy iron straps; ashore, the board would weigh about half a ton, but under water it would have a negative weight. The regular practice to transport a leeboard was to pull it up flat under the fourteen foot barge boat using the slip-ropes John had referred to, and then simply scull or row it away. Thus we travelled the mile and a half back to **Memory** at Mill Beach. With the runner hooked into the preventer link, and the vang shackled onto the tail iron, it was then possible to pull the leeboard alongside and into position. By this time the tide was well away, and we only just managed to get off the mooring and find deeper water. What a way to start a weekend; nevertheless we made Burnham.

The barge struggled on; John was also making business contacts, and secured a five-year contract with the Redbridge Education Authority to charter the barge for their sole use. This was just what John needed, and he promptly gave notice in from his shore job to become permanent skipper of the **Memory** in the forthcoming season. He then approached me and said, "Why don't you find yourself a barge so that you can take on the **Memory**'s 'rough stuff' work?" This was his description of the clientele he had been getting. He made it clear however that I would have to take on his 'permanent staff' as he was eager to get rid of most of them.

The **Lord Roberts** seemed an ideal opportunity for me, but she lacked the agility of most of the barges I had shipped aboard before.

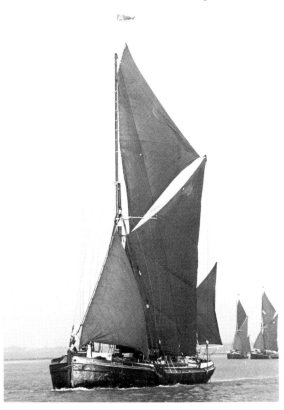

At this time, Tony Winter had been doing a bit of part-time chartering over in Kent, in an ad-hoc fashion, with the **Lord Roberts**, and therefore didn't have a permanent skipper. As I wanted to get back into sail full-time, I went and saw Tony and put the suggestion to him that I should take the barge on and operate from Maldon, with the small amount of work that he'd secured, and with the bulk of the work that Sid Budd was finding. Tony agreed to this, and both of us being familiar with the barge tradition for squaring up, we agreed that we should sail without a mate and use the charterers as crew, and that the proceeds of the charter fee should be split in a manner very similar to the old-fashioned system from the days of cargo carrying. Tony would take 60% of the gross earnings and pay owner's expenses, and I would take 40% of the gross. This meant that we both had an increase on the old-fashioned method, and I think it was equally fair. Under the share system neither of us had an assured income from the barge, which provided an incentive to make it successful.

The season of 1965 saw me chartering the **Lord Roberts** out of Maldon and gradually building up what was eventually to become a successful charter business. Tony and I got on extremely well together; we were both interested in me coming in as a share-owning partner, but unfortunately the **Lord Roberts** was still under-capitalised, and try as I may I could not really take to her.

She'd been built by Cook's of Maldon, who were only interested in carrying capacity, and in no way could she be described as elegant. One day I heard somebody remark sarcastically to one of her previous skippers, "Who designed your barge, Bob - Camper and Nicholson?" She was a big old lumpy thing with blunt ends, and was probably under-rigged. She was so utterly slow; she seemed to stand in the same hole all the time, and she failed to inspire me at all after my time in the **Memory**. I spent hours and hours doing maintenance work, but even with the help of the 'permanent staff' was not able to get her up to the standard that I wished. To give her a bit more appeal, 'Tubs' and I burnt all the tar off in our spare time and gave her sides a coat of grey paint with black above.

We did most of this whilst laying on Sadd's buoy in the reach off Heybridge Basin. We were well exposed to the wind; some days it was impossible to keep the Calor gas blowlamps from blowing out, so we reverted to an old-fashioned method. In those days they used to sell pipkins of beer, which were in fact a gallon tin. We saved one of these, cut a letterbox slot along one side and nailed the whole thing onto a broken oar handle. We then stuffed the tin with rags saturated in diesel oil. When you put a match to this, the pressure in the pipkin got so high that the flames roared out and the more the wind blew, the fiercer would be the heat. In fact it got so hot that we found the way to do this was for one to hold the home-made burner, and the other to use a long-handled scraper. We discovered this was far more efficient than the blowlamps.

With Sid Budd's help, we kept fairly busy during the 1965 season, and with a party of seventeen from the London School of Music, we made a voyage to Snape, where the Maltings was just being fitted out as a concert hall. We were the first barge back for twenty-seven years, and 'Jumbo' Ward, the old-time pilot, huffled us up. We had several nice days there, and when it was time to come away, George Gooderham, the owner of the Maltings, laid on most of the village to take the trip down the river as far as Slaughden. Being country folk, it was like having a harvest festival as they all came aboard bringing bagfulls of

their homemade garden produce such as carrots, potatoes and greens, etcetera. With our seventeen charterers, and Jumbo Ward together with his wife, we made our way down to Slaughden Quay, where the press came on board to a proper East Coast night of singing, which gave us much publicity in the newspapers.

Unfortunately the Yarmouth Board of Trade official, on reading of our numbers on board, sent out an immediate search for us. However, we'd already left Slaughden Quay and were miles at sea by the time he arrived. Our next landfall was the East Swale. We were having a really great time until, at 11 p.m., Tony Winter arrived on board in a very agitated state, as the Board of Trade man had located him at The London and Rochester Trading Company's office at Strood. It looked as if we might be for the high jump because, added to this, the Darlwyn, a pleasure boat, had recently foundered on the south coast and unfortunately people had been drowned. Tony ordered that the number on board be reduced to 12 immediately, which turned out to be 7 a.m. the next morning, and I had to take the barge to Rochester to take on extra life-saving equipment together with a 16' lifeboat fitted with buoyancy tanks.

Jumbo Ward, Tony Winter and me on our way up to Snape aboard **Lord Roberts**.

The charterers, when hearing that some of them would have to be put ashore, were very sporting, and enough of them volunteered to get the numbers down. I was in a worse position, as I'd got my wife and one-year-old daughter on board, and in my haste and concern I forgot to give them any money to get home from Hollowshore to Brightlingsea, which was about a six hour journey at best. Once at Rochester, with the extra lifesaving equipment on board and this huge 16' lifeboat, and our numbers reduced, the Board of Trade man on finding us seemed much appeased and I think a lot of his good humour must be credited to Tony Winter's clever P.R. work.

The Whitsun bank holiday saw us enter for both the Medway and Southend barge matches. We knew we didn't stand much chance of taking a place, but the races always appealed to the charterers in those days. On this occasion, the Medway race took place first. We were laid at anchor off Gillingham when the **Memory** arrived, and I

The **Lord Roberts** racing during her chartering days.

remember Pauline saying to me, "Look at that, Jim, she's the loveliest looking barge here." She was still my favourite barge, and with a twinge of regret I wished that she was still mine. She did indeed make the most handsome sight in the fleet that bank holiday.

The start of the race next morning was very fine; the **Memory** unfortunately drifted in amongst the yachts on the Gillingham shore and got aground. We in the **Lord Roberts** completed the course but came home last, and as we came up to the finish, **Memory** was only just coming afloat to come and anchor and join us in the evening's prize-giving and entertainment.

The next race was at Southend two days later, the conditions being a brisk easterly. Our result was much the same; **Memory** was one of the few barges to carry her staysail in the ever freshening wind, and unfortunately carried away her topmast as a result. The following day, with the wind still fresh easterly, there were four of us barges bound back to Maldon. We were all under way before high water and started for home. The **Lord Roberts**, with her snug rig, was at her best in these conditions, and with mainsail, topsail, foresail and mizzen, was able to keep her sails full in the lumpy seas. **Memory** was, of course, not so fortunate, being without her topmast. This meant that her sprit lunged to windward, and jerking back to leeward, put a lot of weight on the wangs. Rolling wangs would have of course solved this problem, but yacht barges hadn't yet got round to these refinements.

Once below the South Whitaker, I decided not to punch on for the Spitway, but to bear away up the Whitaker and wait for water over the Raysand channel. It was at this time that the **Memory**, being behind us, took an extra lunge and the vang parted. This put all the weight on the leech of the mainsail, and caused it to split from leech to throat. In desperation, they bore away and followed us up the Whitaker channel. Luckily, the **Memory** was far enough below the South Whitaker to find water over the spit.

When I got to the West Buxey, the water was more sheltered, but there was not enough of it to get over the Raysand, so I came to anchor. The **Memory**, her sprit now adrift, the mainsail in two halves and missing her topmast, looked more like the 'Wreck of the Hesperus', a sad sight after what Pauline and I had been praising only a few nights earlier while laying at Gillingham. She anchored under our stern, and John Kemp and Hervey Benham rowed across and asked if I, with the aid of **Lord Roberts**'s engine, would tow them across the Raysand and up to Maldon; this needn't have been said, as no way would I have left them.

With the making of the tide, we got both barges under way. **Lord Roberts** under, topsail, mainsail and foresail and the 66 h.p. Kelvin, with the **Memory** astern. Away we went across the Raysand and saved our tide to Maldon. The next day, young Derby Stebbings, seeing the plight of the **Memory**, informed us that he'd seen Dixon Kerley take in to stock six trees that might be suitable for making into topmasts. With this information, John Kemp sprang into action, and laid on two very special shipwrights, Cecil Wright and Baden Dedman. A few of us went up and selected one of the poles, which was brought onto Maldon quay; John Kemp laid on a barrel of beer and some bread and cheese, those two stalwart shipwrights started hacking out the new topmast whilst all the rest of us helped sort out the barge, getting her mainsail ashore etcetera. The new topmast was actually shipped and hove aloft within twenty-four hours, a sterling effort.

One of our favourite voyages was a trip round Radio Caroline, the pirate radio ship, and even the oldies in the charter parties thought it was exciting to be on the verge of lawbreaking. We would sail right close and shy a request aboard the ship as we went flying past, having put one in an empty Marvel milk tin weighted with a piece of coal (we always used powdered milk as we had no refrigerator on board). The pirate disc jockeys always co-operated in this as it helped to fill up their day and took away some of their boredom. Soon after they got our message, you would hear coming over the airwaves the voice of the D.J. saying, "Hi, Lord Roberts! for the guys and dolls on the barge, here's the tune you requested…" To have their request played gave the charterers the sense of having been somewhere in the voyage, and they hoped all their mates at home would be tuned in at the appropriate time.

We were popular with the charterers when we sailed close by Radio Caroline, their favourite pop songs broadcast over the 'pirate' airwaves.

On one occasion, I had a party of sixth form girls on board, and Tony Blackburn, the well-known D.J. was their idol. A well-prepared message flew across the water, but it fell short and landed in the water just astern of the ship. The radio ship naturally had other crew members on board, and a greaser quickly stripped off his boilersuit and clad only in his under-grundies dived overboard and retrieved the tin. The girls were convinced that this was Tony Blackburn himself; they all laid on the forehatch, their portable radio blaring away, and about fifteen minutes later when their request came floating through the airwaves, they were crying their eyes out, convinced that their hero, Tony, had done this all specially for them.

Our sails were in very bad condition, and I spent quite a lot of time repairing them each trip. But eventually, when off the Eagle[20], bound down to Radio Caroline from the Blackwater, the mainsail blew completely out of its ropes and disappeared over the side. It was all hanging over the rail, and we simply unshackled the tack and the mainsheet, and let it float away. Not a very nice thing to do perhaps, but at least it was all natural fibre and would soon rot away. I then sent a hand aloft to cut the trimmings off the headrope.

A few days after losing our mainsail, Tony informed me that he had booked a honeymoon couple from Belgium to take the barge for the midweek. I said, "But we can't, we've lost the mainsail!" Tony quickly consulted the new bridegroom, who was a real sailing barge devotee and agreed to come anyway; we did the whole honeymoon voyage without it. I was frustrated by the lack of a mainsail and kept trying to make things sound more exciting

[20] The Eagle - A navigation buoy marking the starboard side of the channel into the Blackwater and River Colne.

A mug of tea was most bargemen's start to the morning, repeated now and again or more often throughout the day! This is me in summer, fair weather gear, when chartering.

than they were. I was sad for him because we couldn't make it a very interesting week really, and I've often wondered since, the marriage having got off to such a bad start, did it succeed. I hope so. This was how the season ended, and the mainsail was never replaced.

I told Tony of my misgivings, and we both decided that we could go forward, but with a different barge. It was about this time when Alan Pipe, who owned the Marjorie, came onto the quay one day all agitated, shouting, "I have to sell **Marjorie**! Harold Wilson decrees that I have to sell **Marjorie**!!" Harold Wilson was the Prime Minister and leader of the Labour Party at the time; he had curtailed building in London, and ordered the banks to foreclose on loans. It was a cruel time, and companies were put out of business overnight. John Kemp enquired of Pipe why must he sell **Marjorie**, and he rang out a second time, "Because Harold Wilson decrees that I must sell her! I build office blocks in London and Harold Wilson says no more office blocks, therefore Harold Wilson decrees that I must sell Marjorie!!!"

Tony and I, on hearing this, set up a meeting with Alan Pipe with a view to us purchasing the Marjorie from him, but we soon realised that Pipe was just letting off steam and did not intend (or need) to sell the **Marjorie**. I think that Tony was getting a bit despondent at this time, and he decided to sell the **Lord Roberts**. This left me thinking about a barge for the next season, and as I had built up many contacts I didn't want to see it all come to nothing. It was about Christmas of that year when Pipe came to see me and said, "As you're not chartering in the **Lord Roberts** next year, why don't you take the **Marjorie**?" I said that I had got a nice lot of forward bookings to take with me, but I would only take it on the proviso that if he did sell, I should have first refusal on the purchase of the barge. He said, "Yes, Jim, I promise you that - and on very favourable terms." With this promise, I went ahead for the next season on the same terms as I had had with Tony.

The **Marjorie** was a very fine barge, for which I had great respect. With the nice bit of goodwill that we had made up with the **Lord Roberts**, things looked encouraging for the forthcoming season. She was very well-kept, but she had one failing - she was beginning to leak badly. Search as we may, we could find no apparent reason for this. Alan Pipe even had his doctor on board and together they went over the hull meticulously with the doctor's stethoscope while she was afloat. We all laughed at this because we'd never seen anything like it.

My wife Pauline aboard the **Marjorie**.

Over the years she began to leak more seriously. I remembered a story of when Cook's built a smack called **Souvenir**. When she was launched, she leaked from day one. The yard simply thought they'd drilled a hole for a spike, and omitted to put the spike in, but on taking her ashore, a close inspection showed that this was not the case. Eventually, they got a man in from London who proved that one of the garboards was actually porous, and the water was going in through the fibre of the wood itself. This got me thinking, as each time I scraped the barnacles and weed off the **Marjorie** with a dutch hoe, I noticed that her chines, which were elm, would peel like a carrot. I wondered if the same thing was happening to the **Marjorie** as with the smack. I drove over to Ipswich and sought out Jack Southgate, who was R. & W. Paul's leading shipwright, and put the question to him. "Jack, you've had many years of looking after **Marjorie** during her working life - do you think it is the elm wood that is porous in itself?" Jack immediately said, "Yes, Jim, I think that is the case, and she needs sheathing."

Sheathing was a once-regular means of lengthening a barge's life. It was always done piecemeal, as the capital was never available to do it all in one go, so one year, the chines and middle (keel) range might be sheathed (as we did with the **Marjorie**), then, say a couple of years on, the wales would be sheathed, thus allowing the barge to earn as she went. Eventually the in-between areas would be sheathed with a thinner skin, thus completely 'putting the barge in a box'. Of course it was the 'hair and blair', well payed with tar, that kept the water out.

I put this to Alan Pipe, and said that we should concentrate on sheathing the elm chines and the middle range. He supported the idea immediately, and we looked for a site where we could undertake this work ourselves during the winter months. Pipe, in his exuberance, and with no reference to me, clinched a deal with the new owners of the old Frost and Drake yard at Tollesbury that we could use their slipway for the winter of 1968-9. I was aghast when I went to look at the site. The slipway consisted of two trolleys, both only 16' square, and not much depth of water. This presented a quandary as the barge was 20' wide and 84' long, but Pipe had committed us to it, so I had to take it on from there.

A barge's lateral strength is nearly all contained in the sides, so I had to widen the support on the trolleys to take Marjorie's beam. I did this by putting a series of nineteen foot long baulks across the trolleys, and a further twenty-four foot baulk on top of each of those. As we were going to sheathe under the bottom I then had to put two inch thick pads on top of the longer baulks, which we would be able to take out as we proceeded with the sheathing. Then, to achieve as much longitudinal support as possible, I had to set the trolleys out nineteen foot apart, and secure them to one another with chains. Thus, the barge, when on the trolleys, would have 17'6" overhang forward, 16' on trolley no.1, then a 19' gap, and then trolley no.2 made up another 16', leaving 17'6" overhang aft.

Owing to the lack of water at the foot of the slipway, the trolleys had to be lowered to the bottom of the rails, and closed up together. We then had to float the head of the barge onto trolley no.1, and make her fast to it. Wally, driving the winch (which was the best part of the yard's equipment), now hauled away, with the barge's head slowly coming out the water. As the chains on the trolleys drew tight, trolley no.2 followed behind and the barge eventually settled on the second trolley. We seemed to be doing quite well, and Pipe shouted out, "We're home and dry, Jim!"

Just at that moment, the slipway rails spread apart, leaving the trolleys sitting on the hard and refusing to budge further. We were now in a predicament, as the barge was not yet completely clear of the water and would float on spring tides; it was imperative, as soon as the tide was gone, to lift her sufficiently to allow us to get the trolleys back on the rails. Easier said than done! We hadn't got any jacks, but I had had two hundred elm wedges cut specifically to use during the sheathing process. There were only three of us, and we worked through the night to get the trolleys re-established. I was learning fast. The slipway was badly undermined, and could not really support **Marjorie**'s weight. First, blocks of wood had to be put down in strategic places under the barge, and the barge raised bodily on them with the wedges, then the rails could be jacked back into position, and the barge lowered back down onto the trolleys. The work was long and hard, and it took all the night and until the next day-tide, when the winchman turned up again (along with several onlookers) and on this occasion we were successful.

Once above the spring high water mark, the barge had to be more fully supported at both ends, and as I was advised that the trolleys would settle if the full weight of the barge was left on them during the coming months, it was important to take the weight off them. I then put a string line through the barge to see that she was perfectly straight, and this I repeated every Friday as the beach wasn't entirely stable and adjustments had to be made.

The materials to sheath the barge were 1½" elm, with thick gooey London tar and barge felt between it and the hull. Although the barge was only twenty-eight inches clear of the gravel hard, we had to drill and spike up with 9" spikes into her floors, with 4" spikes in between. The tar, with a handful of pitch added to each gallon of it, had to be heated up and applied to the new plank before offering it up. This was a foul messy job, commonly known as set-work. Each hole had to be drilled, and counter-sunk, and each spike had to be headed-in with a punch. Once the middle range had been completed, we moved on to the bottom chines: then likewise up the side chines, which seemed a doddle in comparison.

One Friday I had a fright. Arthur Holt and myself had been working on the starboard side, and Doug Larsen had been working on the port side, where we'd had the fire for heating the pitch. I called across, "Put the fire out, Doug, we don't want n' more heat today;" and eventually we left for home. It was an hour's trip from

The work progresses on sheathing **Marjorie**'s chines on the Frost & Drake ways at Tollesbury.

Tollesbury to Brightlingsea, and as I drove into James Street where my house was, I went cold - had Doug put the fire out? Without stopping, I drove right past my house and out the other end of the street and all the way back to Tollesbury, and checked. Yes, the fire had been well and truly put out. Doug was such a reliable man, but more wooden ships have been lost through fire, especially when dealing with tar and pitch, so I felt the extra mileage was better than laying awake all night worrying.

The work completed, with a fresh coating of anti-fouling, **Marjorie** awaits rigging out and return to the water.

Arthur, Doug and me made a superb crew, and we all agreed that this was the hardest winter's work we'd ever undertaken. Little did we realise the nightmares were only beginning. The locals came and advised me, "When you want to launch her, boy, you hang a lump of ballast off her bow, and two or three of you pull that back, then let it go and hit the front of the trolley - and watch out, 'cause she'll go down there like a train!"

The day came; we were all ready. She moved three foot before the rails spread, letting the trolleys fall to the beach. Another all-nighter ensued, raising the barge up on blocks with wedges and re-placing the trolleys. We had several more set-to's like this; the dangerous time came as the barge neared the water, and I realised that a spring tide could float her stern and wring her off the trolleys entirely. I decided the time had come to stop the silliness. I sent everyone home, and I spent the next set of neaps entirely working on the rails. I had about twenty pairs of iron grips made up, with a bottlescrew joining each pair, and used these to clamp the rails at their exact spacing apart. They could now move neither off nor in.

As the next set of tides came round, I got Doug and Arthur back, together with some additional help. We had thus far been nine weeks total in launching, and many of our regular charter people were wondering what was holding us up. They made a party up to come to Tollesbury on the very day of the next attempt, and this time we were successful. As the barge slipped back into her natural element at last, I peered down over the side and saw the trolleys completely crumble. I simply laughed; I had got my barge back.

We moored up in the creek as, to complete our contract with the yard, I had to put everything back as I found it - trolleys, huge baulks of wood, etc., and I expected to spend a fortnight clearing up. But the sixty or so charterers that had turned up turned-to immediately, and by five-thirty, the yard was completely cleared and with no sign of the **Marjorie** having been there. What a relief.

I had one more ironic thing to happen. With our very inadequate water-jet power unit, we slowly 'motored' down the creek at three o'clock in the morning, but the tide was so big that I decided to anchor in the Leavings and wait for it to go down a bit, as we could easily have missed the channel and gone onto the saltings. We anchored right in the middle, and whilst we were waiting for the tide to drop, the wind came athwart, and blew the stern out of the gut and up against the salting edge. When I looked out, she was down by the

head, with her stern high and dry. I thought, Well, that's put paid to this tide, and was about to go below again when I noticed her start to slide towards the gutway. I said to Pipe, "Quick - start the engine!" whilst I got the anchor. This made her slip down the mud and relaunch herself, and sent her hurtling down the channel. What a peculiar winter. To take nine weeks launching off a conventional slipway, yet the barge launched herself down the mud.

And so we returned to Maldon to rig out and start our charter work. Surely, this was the hardest winter I'd ever endured, but at least the **Marjorie** never leaked again. She drew 4" less water, through drying out, and was the fastest barge on the Blackwater all that season.

The elm placque made from a sheathing off-cut commemorates this succesful repair, recording the individuals involved, the materials used and when we did it.

We still sailed without a full-time mate, using the charterers as the crew; this enabled me to take my pals away at weekends as the regular mate. They didn't get paid, and they didn't have to pay, but they got their sailing for nothing. That great character, Rick Cardy, first sailed with me when he was a schoolboy, and showed great promise even then. He was thoroughly reliable, but also good with the charterers, and soon developed into a popular storyteller. I was deep into Hornblower in the early days, and Rick would pull the

hatch over and lock me down in the cabin, saying, "Go on, Lawrence, we don't want you up here!" I would have to sit below and read my Hornblower books while he yarned and amused the charterers. I had every confidence in him, and knew the barge was perfectly safe in his young hands.

When people asked me what I preferred, trading with cargoes or sailing in the holiday work, well, I found it difficult to give them an answer. The lonely solitary life with the independence and self-determination of the trading days gave for greater satisfaction, whilst with chartering you had the

The irrepressible Rick Cardy.

opportunity to enjoy and share with many others that which you thought was worthwhile, and the passing on of skills and knowledge has always given me much pleasure.

Kitty in 1955, then 60 years old and still carrying dry cargoes under sail.

Kitty at 120 years old, with a 44 passenger certificate, carrying a very different cargo.

For company, we had the **Kitty**, with John Fairbrother as skipper, also doing the same work, and it is interesting how we built up our own clienteles. Those who booked with John one year would become his loyal patrons for the future, and likewise those who booked with **Marjorie** would stay with her. They really became our friends; I had a light-hearted approach to my charterers, and when one dear little old lady, coming away for

the first time, informed me that she couldn't swim and enquired as to what she should do if the boat sank. I told her that as soon as she hit the bottom she should run like billy-oh, but I soon reassured her of the care and consideration that we put into the job, and of the sailing barges' great safety record.

The accent was on sailing, and we did not stick to a regular route, but would go wherever the wind suited us best. If our judgement was correct hopefully we would have a fair wind home at the end of the voyage. But the cry, on coming aboard, would be, "Where are we going, skip?" "We're going to Gunga Poo!" I would reply, "A place where white man has never before set foot." I spent all my chartering years searching for Gunga Poo, and we never did find it, which proves the point that it is far better to travel hopefully than it is to actually arrive.

In 1968, the City of London decided to replace London Bridge. The new bridge was to be wider and built out of pre-cast concrete, whereas the bridge they were replacing, built in 1832, was Aberdeen grey granite. Whether the old bridge was advertised for sale or not I don't know, but the Yanks, on hearing of this, put in a bid for it. They were successful, and apparently thought they had bought Tower Bridge, or so the story goes; but one lovely feature of the American psyche is they love to be the

Old London Bridge was sold to the U.S.A. and rebuilt at Lake Havasu, Arizona.

butt of a joke, and they went along with it anyway. They never intended to take the entire London Bridge to America but, having built a replica London Bridge in the Arizona Desert and digging a river afterwards, were only going to cut four inch thick slabs off the original and stick them on their own bridge as though they were tiles. A picture clearly shows London Bridge installed in America with the Nevada Mountains in the background.

In the meantime, Mowlem's, who were dismantling the old structure, were also busy encapsulating small pieces of the stone in blocks of clear resin, and together with a certificate of provenance, were selling pieces of London Bridge off at £5 a time; they were going like hot cakes. In fact, the residue of the old bridge amounted to many thousands of tons, and this was shipped round the coast by The London and Rochester Trading Company's motor barges to the River Crouch, supposedly to build up the sea wall. I was a bit disgusted when it wasn't actually built into the wall, but just dumped off at the foot of it, where it might do a little good, but for the main part was a waste. So, when the wallers finished work, I took about three tons of the stone on board the **Marjorie** and took it home; my father-in-law built himself a grand rockery in his front garden, all with beautiful Aberdeen granite, which was the pride of the whole road.

Each year, in the early and latter parts of the season, we would only get bookings for weekends, leaving the mid-weeks clear to do maintenance. John Fairbrother and I both decided to make a new pair of leeboards. John made his on Maldon quay, whereas I had a site in Blackwater Timber Co.'s wood yard at nearby Heybridge Basin, and whilst we selected a slightly different design, they were very much based on the old traditional pattern with no view to the modern aerofoil that is sometimes employed today.

For the **Marjorie**'s, we were able to locate a large oak tree in Framlingham, Suffolk, which caused a small outburst from the locals, but when I visited the village, and showed them a picture of the barge and what we intended to do with the tree, all was quietly accepted. The wood yard sliced the tree up into three inch planks, eighteen inches wide, and after I had shaped them up I laid them on forty-five gallon oil barrels and cramped them all together. The local Goldhanger blacksmith, George Emeny, supplied me with the ironwork, and then came the rub. In those days it was impossible to find the iron to make up the rivets, and only steel nuts and bolts were available.

So we went ahead in the following manner: I bolted the straps and the board together, using the head of the bolt into the wood, and the nut screwed tightly on the pre-drilled ironwork, one hundred and forty-four bolts in all between the pair of them. When the boards had been bolted together and hove tight, I informed Emeny and one Sunday, three of them appeared. Putting a lorry jack under each bolt head in turn, and lightly taking the weight of the leeboard, we would remove the nut and heat the threaded end with a blowtorch; they could then rivet it securely into the countersunk hole in the iron bands. Thus we were improving the performance of our barges. I also made the **Marjorie** a new topmast, and replaced a rotted quarterboard. Some were small tasks, others much bigger, but all helped keep these aging craft up to scratch.

I was never able to save any capital whilst chartering with **Marjorie**, but was still hoping to buy her if Alan Pipe concluded that he should sell. I decided that if this came about, I would put the proposition to a few of my regular charterers with a view to forming a club, as owning the barge itself wasn't my main interest so much as carrying on with the way of life. However, I did find that she was being advertised for sale in glossy magazines, and I came to the conclusion that Pipe thought he would get more for her as a private yacht rather than as a charter barge. The original agreement no longer seemed to be on offer.

Another passion of mine was sailmaking, and I was getting many orders for sails which I was hand-making on board; with a small fisherman's store as a loft in Brightlingsea, this had become my regular winter work. Little did I know that I was about to embark on a business venture that would lead me into full-time sailmaking.

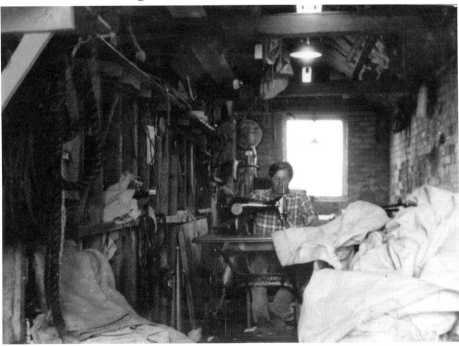

The tiny fisherman's store that was my first 'sail loft' had barely enough room for me, the sewing machine and the sailcloth.

Chapter XXIII

A Stitch in Time

I had spent seven very contented years chartering, first in the **Lord Roberts** and then in the **Marjorie**. When people asked me what I preferred, trading with cargoes or sailing in the holiday work, well, I found it difficult to give them an answer. The lonely solitary life with the independence and self-determination of the trading days gave for greater satisfaction. With chartering you had the opportunity to enjoy and share with many others that which you thought was worthwhile, and the passing on of skills and knowledge has always given me much pleasure. The **Marjorie** was not going to be available to me for the 1971 season so I had to find another barge, or think of something else to support my family.

I had always kept my hand in with the sail repairs needed for the barges, and also had plenty of orders for sails to get me through the winter of 1971. Across the road from my home in Brightlingsea was a shop called 'Babyland', run by a Mrs. Little. As the shop name suggests, it sold baby clothes, prams and pushchairs, etc. She had decided to retire and put the property up for sale. The building inside measured 19 x 48 feet, not a bad size for a sail loft, I thought. Mrs. Little was all for me having it and set a very reasonable price.

In the meantime I got in touch with a government assistance scheme called CoSIRA[21]. They offered me practical help together with an attractive loan. The only money I could raise was selling my lovely old smack **Rosena** for £700. I found a worthy buyer in one named Max Monsarrat whose dad was the author Nicholas Monsarrat of 'The Cruel Sea' fame.

However, I was not yet totally set on it, as I still craved a barge. In the meantime someone tried to gazump me by offering Mrs. Little a lot more money. That good lady said an emphatic "NO! It's Jim's, and if he can get the money it is his". I thought, what a lovely thing for her to do, and using this as an omen I immediately went to the solicitors and signed up. I have never looked back.

21. *C.o.S.I.R.A. - the Council of Small Industries in Rural Areas.*

I was now committed to full-time sailmaking and really expected to be working entirely alone, when Stephen Swann approached me. Just starting out on a journalistic career with the magazine Yachts and Yachting, Stephen asked, "Cor, Jim, can I come and work for you?" "No," said I, "I'm afraid not, I would not be able to find you a wage." The following weekend Stephen called round to my house and said, "I have given my notice in. I shall be starting with you next month and will wait until enough money is coming in before I expect to get any wages."

Stephen, with a consortium of his pals, had bought the cut-down and motorised bawley **Bona** and was giving her a rebuild. Just previous to my going into full-time sailmaking, I had researched and made for them a suit of working sails in Royal Navy flax. This really was the start of something new, as no bawley had been rigged in the last forty years.

My smack **Rosena**, before recommissioned, **Memory** beyond.

Her charter party carries **Kitty**'s new mainsail down the Brightlingsea Hard causeway. It is much lighter when new, before dressing. A barge's 'rig' - spars, dressed sails, ropes and blocks weigh in at around 5 tons!

One of Stephen's last articles for Yachts and Yachting was entitled 'Rebirth of a Bawley'. Stephen really was welcome on board, and soon earned his keep.

The work soon poured in and before long we were urgently looking for a third person, who came in the shape of John Wright, a former tailor. It is not that I wanted to be an entrepreneur, but because I wanted to provide a complete service to my rapidly growing portfolio of customers.

A demonstration of traditional sailmaking.

One day Lew Foweraker, a good friend of mine, well-known in the barge world, telephoned me. He was a member of the Upnor Royal Engineers Yacht Club, and said, "Jim, do you want a really huge sewing machine?" He went on to explain that the Army were clearing a certain building and that everything had to be dumped because they had no means of selling anything. I hadn't got much in the way of sewing machines, and did not expect this offering to be much better. Anyhow, I said that I would drive over the next day to look at it.

When I got to the club the following morning, Lew showed me the machine, which had had hardly any use. It was out of this world, and would have cost many hundreds of pounds to purchase new. Lew said, "What do you think?" "It's wonderful," said I. "Well," said Lew, "if you go into that office and see the officer in charge, it's yours. All you have got to do is put £20 in the tea caddy."

My feet hardly touched the ground as I charged into the office, but was brought-up short. The officer in charge was a woman, immaculate in her tight-fitting uniform, close cropped hair and steely dark eyes. I felt like a squaddie; I did not know whether to curtsy or salute, so I did both! In spite of my gymnastics she took my money and the machine became mine. It did Trojan work for many years - well done Lew.

The sails were getting bigger and bigger. Dominic Jones with the Baltic trader **Gray**, and Dr. Leslie Morrish with the beautiful **Irene** of Bridgewater were two of my first orders, and both men have remained firm and special friends.

Geoff Mellor owned the **Ethel Ada**, the Paglesham one[22]. He had just bought a suit of second-hand sails from John Kemp, ex-**Thalatta**. They were full of thick gooey sail dressing, and the mainsail needed cutting down. "Can you do it for me, Jim?" he asked. "Well, yes," said I, but I was apprehensive of all that sticky

Vigilent, showing off her new mainsail we made from No.2 Royal Navy flax.

[22] *Ethel Ada* - two sailing barges of this name were engaged in similar trades at the same time, one built at Paglesham, Essex, on the River Roach by Shuttlewoods, the other built at Ipswich by Horace Shrubsall.

sail dressing. It was bound to get everywhere in my smart new sail loft. "Leave it with me," I said, wondering how I was going to tackle the problem. Then I had a flash of inspiration - the weather forecast for the next day was good; sunny and dry. I sent Stephen and John home early telling them to return at 6.30 a.m.; then I got to work.

James Street, where the loft was situated, is a short road adjoining two that run down to the Waterside, namely New Street and Sydney Street. Since there were other roads that did the same thing I reckoned that closing James Street wouldn't put anybody out. I had plenty of 4" x 2" timbers and with these I made up two 'road closed' signs. I gave them a coat of magnolia emulsion paint and then stencilled on B.U.D.C. ROAD CLOSED.

Sure enough, at 6.30 a.m. prompt we put the signs up, one at each end of James Street, and spread the mainsail out in order to let the sun warm and soften the canvas. Then we got stuck in. During the day several cars tried to turn into James Street but, as soon as they saw the road closed, they simply backed out and took one of the alternative routes, leaving us to work uninterrupted all day.

When Geoff came to pick the mainsail up at 4 p.m. it was ready for him. I had reopened the road and my precious sail loft was still

The sail loft frontage overlooks a large forecourt, ideal for sail dressing, when the weather serves.

clean. All that was needed now were for three Red Indians to go home for a bath to scrub the sail dressing off.

We needed more room, and found this in a building that was formerly the Foresters' Hall. This meant a really huge commitment from me. I was about to turn it down, when Hazel Grey, my then secretary, shuffled a large amount of quotes in her hands and exclaimed, "Come on, don't let's lose all this lovely work." Once again, on impulse, I went straight to the solicitors and signed up. The Foresters' Hall was in quite a dilapidated state when I first moved in, and took many years of ploughing money into it to get it to the standard that I wished it to be. We did achieve this, thanks in great measure to my dear friend Jack Carpenter, who very quickly got the electrics back on and then spent the next fourteen years coming one day a week looking after the maintenance. Although Jack made it his social day out, his time was all free of charge. They don't make many like Jack.

We were getting quite a lot of work with the barges, and I felt that I had support and encouragement from the other barge sailmakers, Fred Taylor of Maldon, Alf Naylor, Sid Butler and the Whitstable loft's Mr. Goldfinch, always referred to, though I don't know why, as Mr. Goldfinch, and never by his Christian name Ray.

Inside the Tower Street sail loft, miles of twine, line and sailcloth are ready for hand sewing or machine work.

Our sails for the **Søren Larsen** have travelled the oceans of the world. As well as appearing on screen in The Onedin Line, The French Lieutenant's Woman and Shackleton, she continues her role as a sail-training ship, based in Australia.

Despite not giving too much away, as they were all about to retire, they were very generous with their knowledge. Perhaps they felt, like me, that they wanted their skills to go on. The man that I am most indebted to is Percy Gladwell of J.O. Whitmore Ltd., the sailmakers and ships chandlers on the dockside at Ipswich, who joined that firm when he was thirteen years old. His name was really Jack, but the master sailmaker at that time was also named Jack. "We can't have two Jacks," they exclaimed, "so you will have to be Percy." and the name stuck. In the early days I used to buy my sailcloth from Whitmore, and when they packed up and Percy retired, he would keep his hand in by doing a few jobs at home. He would come to Brightlingsea and buy his cloth from me; what a pal and a gentleman.

By this time we were making sails for the big square-riggers that were now coming back into popularity. Among these were the **Esther Lohse** which starred in the Onedin Line television series. There was also the brigantine **Søren Larsen**, which we rigged out to be a sail-training ship for the able and disabled under the flag of the Jubilee Sailing Trust, whilst owned by Square Sail of Charlestown, Cornwall. She then became the flag ship of the First Fleet Re-enactment, which was to commemorate the first convict fleet to Australia two hundred years before.

Next came the **Lord Nelson**, custom-built for the Jubilee Sailing Trust and **Kaskelot** which has starred in TV and film.

The **Lord Nelson** was designed and built especially to accommodate and allow the less physically able to experience the comradeship and teamwork of a sailing ship with square rig.

Sea Cloud is no longer a private yacht, but a cruise ship providing a most unique and luxurious holiday experience. Setting 30 sails on three masts, this was an order that represented quite a challenge for the loft.

Sea Cloud is one of the world's largest sailing yachts and is owned by a German shipping company. She was a four-masted barque, built in 1931 as a wedding present for the American heiress Marjorie Merriweather Post. She passed through many changes of ownership before being bought by a German consortium who operate her as a luxury cruise ship in the Caribbean and Mediterranean. She sets a total of 32,000 square feet of canvas in her 30 sails, both exciting and a bit daunting for us. Amongst her many crew over the years, one girl, Lucy Harris, was sailmaker aboard her, and subsequently came to Brightlingsea to work in our sail loft.

There were quite a lot more, and we prided ourselves on being able to tackle anything to do with ships, whether it be sails, rigging or awnings. We had our highs, but it wasn't all beer and skittles. The 1980s proved a very hard time, with companies going down like ninepins. Francis Webster of Arbroath was my biggest supplier of flax canvas. Getting a knighthood for his inventive talents and in business since 1717, in 1795 they perfected the art of adding linseed oil to flax sails, creating an oiled flax with much a improved performance over previous sailcloths. Adopted by the Royal Navy and commercially for the tea clippers, the firm became the largest sailcloth producers in the world.

Suddenly, in the mid 1980s, I heard that they had the receivers in, and had stopped production. This threw me into a panic - if I could not get sail cloth how could I stay in business myself? Fortunately, the receiver telephoned me saying that they had plenty of ready-made stock, and if I took the whole quantity I could have it for a very good price. In the middle of a deep recession, with interest rates at 15%, I was in a quandary as to what to do? Well, five of us needed a living, so I went to the bank and asked for a huge overdraft. The bank fortunately backed me, and this gave me a lot of confidence to come through those hard times leaner and stronger.

All the young people who came to me to learn sailmaking are still working at it and passing on the knowledge that was made freely available to me. It is a great comfort to me to know that traditional sailmaking is still very much alive and thriving.

My Merchant Navy British Seaman's Identity Card issued at the Mercantile Marine Office, Colchester, on 6th December 1948.

It is a long way from the days of the Wilson Marriage 'Apprehensive' School, and the issue of my Merchant Navy Identity Card to me, complete with dubious portrait photograph, at the age of fifteen.

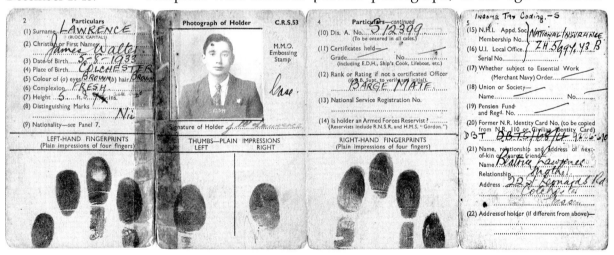

The Royal Hospital School at Holbrook.

However, this led directly to my grandchildren being granted bursaries to attend as boarders at one of our finest schools in Suffolk, namely the Royal Hospital School at Holbrook, with its magnificent views of the Mistley River. No doubt I could never have foreseen this possibility back in the 1950s when I joined the sailing barge **Gladys** as third hand.

Chapter XXIV

The 'Violent Helen'

Once I had made the break and decided to settle down ashore, I got to thinking about a vessel for myself and this came along in a partnership in the bawley **Helen & Violet**. Johnny Welch, a farmer, was her owner, simply as a cut-down motor fishing vessel, and that was to be his contribution.

Cyril White, a renowned Brightlingsea boat builder, took on the responsibility of putting her hull back into pristine condition, whilst my contribution was to provide all the sails, rigging and cordage. She was to be renovated in a totally traditional manner and with no engine. When this stage had been reached, we were then considered to be equal partners. It proved to be an amicable partnership that reigned for fourteen years.

It took four years to get her back into commission under sail and we could see right away that she was a flier, well, at least downwind, that is. As soon as we came on the wind the mast went all shapes and she would not stand to windward. This was a big disappointment, but we had to bite the bullet. A bawley mast had to be so much stiffer than a smack's mast. We were learning fast.

Cyril had a contact in Bow Creek who imported forty-foot long pines, fourteen inches square. So Cyril and I joined the commuters on the 8.45 a.m. to London. Looking down at the floor of the train, I noticed that Cyril's boots looked odd. I said, "That's strange, Cyril, you have got one brown boot and one black boot." "There is nothing strange about that," he drawled and, you've guessed it, "I've got another pair at home exactly the same!"

On the way to the timber yard we got slightly lost and had to ask the way to Robinson Road. "What, do you want the Social Security Office?" asked our helpful Londoner. "No;" replied Cyril, "I don't think things are as bad as that yet."

Once at the office of the timber merchant it was sheer delight. They loved timber and they knew right away that Cyril loved timber too. We went into the yard, and Cyril had five baulks turned over before he found the one that he wanted. They certainly recognised a kindred spirit. With the business done, the boss fetched his Bentley to the front office and drove us back to the railway station.

The bawley **Helen & Violet** shows the power of the genre. Often thought the poor relation compared with the smack hull form in terms of performance, but a few of the type proved able to put the smacks in the shade when racing.

With her new mast, **Helen & Violet** sailed like a witch, not quite as close-winded as the smacks, but let her have her head and she would travel through the water so fast that she would come out ahead every time. She soon became known as the 'Violent Helen', and remained top boat for the remaining nine years that we were together.

Perhaps the best times were our weekend cruises to Paglesham or Stangate Creek, listening to the many stories related to us by Cyril and Jack Cook. Cyril portrayed himself as rough and ready, but was recognised as a very fine shipwright and boat builder and his Folkboats were especially renowned. However, he had been educated at Oundle Public School. Frank Thompson coined the phrase, "Cyril was the only man to run a successful business where the customer was always wrong; but they loved him for it."

Jack Cook, on the other hand, was born with a plastic spoon in his mouth. His dad had been a yacht skipper; Jack followed him, going to sea in yachts serving titled gentry. Jack had been torpedoed whilst serving in the North Atlantic convoys and had been machine-gunned while struggling in the freezing water. He was the oldest crew member, but his humour and youthfulness kept everyone young,

The B.B.C. chose **Helen & Violet** to star in one of their 'Old Gaffers' series. They pitted us against the smack **Sunbeam**. Our sail loft had only just fitted her out, so it was rather tongue-in-cheek to think that we had got to race against her. This could be a bit embarrassing as we would surely race at our hardest. Well, perhaps it was lucky for us that **Sunbeam** went ashore during the race so that there was no contest between us. Our lovely **Helen & Violet** went on home to take the cup - what happy memories that day made for us.

After fourteen very happy years, we brought our partnership to an end. This was because Johnny wanted to retire and live full time aboard the **Helen & Violet**; Cyril wanted to sail his Folkboat **Scandal** more often. Scandal was a clever play on words as it is the fastest thing to get around Brightlingsea. I had bought the very beautiful **Lily May**, a King's Lynn smack, from Barry Tester at Hollowshore. All very amicable.

The smack **Lily May** shows off her lines on Brightlingsea hard.

The bawley **Saxonia**.

Unfortunately for me, and still with some regrets, as soon as I got **Lily May** home, a consortium of people from our local yacht club wanted to buy her from me so, as I was still bawley-crazy, I sold her and went and bought the bawley **Saxonia**. Well, she was no flier and would never match the **Helen & Violet**, but she did make an excellent day charter vessel, and as I loved meeting people this is what I fitted her out for. I built her up into a very good business before eventually retiring and passing her on.

Another skill that I wanted to keep alive was my barge racing, and when Simon Devonshire asked me to skipper his **Marjorie** I was well pleased. I then spent eleven pleasurable years racing and sailing with Simon and his crew from Hoo, near Rochester. We started off by coming home in the middle of the fleet but soon got her up to be a high contender and taking many wins.

I have a very special affection for the sailing barge **Marjorie**, as between us Mick Lungley, Pat Fisher and myself had spent so much time working with her. In Simon she has a very good owner and skipper.

Maritime author and owner of the tremendously successful Essex County Newspaper Group, Hervey Benham, once said that you start off with a small boat, then you go onto bigger boats and finally you come back to little boats again. Well, that's true of me. I now sail

185

Marjorie, which I skippered that day, on her way to second place in the 2006 Colne Smack and Barge Race, beaten by the all-conquering **Edme**.

My **Native.**

my 17 foot lug-rig **Native**, and I have the best mate in the world in my wife Pauline. We sail locally now, but always seek out the old barge quays such as at Mersea Strood where Tubby Blake in his **Lancashire** took many a cargo of Kentish ragstone for rebuilding the sea walls.

Also there is 'Toozey' Mill (St. Osyth), Thorrington Mill, Fingringhoe Mill, where a big tree laying across the creek stops you getting that last half-mile. Last, but not least, is the Hythe at Colchester, and of course Marriage's East Mills. We have our mast in a mast-case so that she is easy to lower down. We don't take on a huffler these days, but if old Brownie turned up on his bike I would be more than pleased to give him a tide's work.

I have been under sail and oar most of my life but last year I relented and bought Pauline an outboard motor for her birthday! She was fed up with having to row home on calm evenings.

"I'll see you!"

INDEX

Vessel names are in bold type. Page numbers in italics indicate illustrations/caption text; page numbers followed by 'n' refer to footnotes.

Index prepared by James Helling of
Shorehan, West Sussex.
jameshellingindexer@gmail.com